Devotional Talks
for People Who Do
God's Business

Devotional Talks for People Who Do God's Business

David W. Wiersbe
and
Warren W. Wiersbe

BAKER BOOK HOUSE
Grand Rapids, Michigan 49506

Contents

Introduction

I must give the devotions at the next committee meeting, and I don't know what to say!"

It is our hope that the messages in this book will help to solve that problem. They are designed to encourage people who are involved in God's work and are suitable for use in a variety of settings within the church organization.

You certainly can use these messages for your own personal enrichment. You can take time to assimilate them and eventually share them in your own words with others. Or you might even want to read a pertinent chapter to your board or committee, if you feel that's the best way to get the message across.

In any event, our prayer is that these devotional talks will help you in your own spiritual life and, through you, help to prosper the Christian work in which you are involved. These messages have been used with blessing in local church situations, and we offer them for this wider ministry with the prayer that Christ will thereby be glorified and his church edified.

David W. Wiersbe
Warren W. Wiersbe

1

The Kind of Leaders God Needs
Exodus 18:13–26

Moses was a gifted man, and yet he was unable to handle all the duties of leadership that came to him each day. We know that he was an educated man (Acts 7:22) and dedicated wholly to God, but still he could not accomplish everything the people expected of him. Moses needed help, and he received that help in the form of men assigned to oversee the work with him. God did not solve Moses' problems by performing miracles. He just gave him associates who helped to carry the load.

While it is true that the church is an "organism," it is equally true that an organism must be organized or it will die: "Let all things be done decently and in order" (1 Cor. 14:40). However, if taking care of the church's organization becomes more important to us than the ministry itself, we then have an "institution," and we are in trouble. If we remember to use the organization to get God's work done, then God will bless it.

What kind of helpers—officers—did God give Moses to share the work of the Lord and help carry the load? They are described in verse 21 of this passage.

To begin with, they were "people," ordinary human beings, called by God to get the job done. No doubt God could have sent angels, but he deigned to choose common people to do this important work. These associates had their weaknesses and faults, and perhaps there were times when Moses disagreed with them. Life is always like that. We must learn to accept each other as individuals, love each other, and work together to get the job done and tackle our mutual concerns.

Have you ever considered the problems our Lord's apostles may have had in working together? Simon was a Zealot before Jesus called him, which meant that Simon was out to destroy the power of Rome. But Matthew had been a tax collector, an employee of the Romans! James and John had such short fuses that Jesus called them "sons of thunder" (Mark 3:17), and Peter was anything but timid. The apostles were ordinary people, each of them different; yet Jesus was able to unite them and get his work accomplished.

These helpers were also "able," people who knew what they were meant to do and had the potential to do it well. No amount of sincerity or dedication can compensate for a person's lack of ability. It is tragic when the church is insensitive to this fact and gives its members tasks that they cannot perform. Each of us has certain abilities and spiritual gifts, and we must serve in that place where these talents will count the most.

These people were to "fear God." Moses would not be able to watch all of them work or listen to all of them give counsel, but God would be listening and watching. When servants of God truly fear God, they will not fear anything else. They will make decisions that please the Lord, even if those deci-

10

sions cost them popularity. It is not easy to be in a position of authority and ministry, but we make that place even harder if we forget the fear of the Lord.

To fear God also means to worship him. It is so important that those who lead God's work spend time each day in God's presence. A consistent daily devotional life—reading the Word, praying, and seeking God's face—is essential for God's blessing in spiritual leadership.

Another important quality that these assistants possessed was that they were "men of truth." They spoke truth and hated lies. The spiritual bonds that hold the church together are truth and love: "...speaking the truth in love" (Eph. 4:15). It has well been said that love without truth is hypocrisy, and truth without love is brutality. We cannot allow either hypocrisy or brutality in our church. Sometimes the truth does hurt, but if we speak that truth in love, we apply the spiritual medicine that helps to heal any wounds we have inflicted.

The final characteristic listed is "hating covetousness." Since Moses' assistants occasionally served as judges in civil cases, they no doubt were offered bribes, and they had to learn to say no. Church leaders today are not as likely to be offered bribes, but a person can be covetous of other things beside money—popularity, the approval of certain people, recognition, even power and authority.

This matter of covetousness also touches us in our own personal stewardship. A church leader ought to be generous in giving. We ought to set the example. It is not right for us to process the sacrificial gifts of other people if we ourselves are not

11

bountiful givers. God sees our hearts and knows what is there.

No church officer is perfect, but each should strive to be the best leader possible. Would God have chosen you and me as leaders if we had lived in Moses' day? I hope so!

Where we turn for counsel is good evidence of what kind of guidance we really want. Certainly the wise old men who had counseled Solomon knew what to advise the young king, but Rehoboam preferred to listen to the advice of his young friends. Perhaps it was "peer pressure" that made him reject the wisdom of the experienced counselors. Or perhaps he had decided beforehand what advice he wanted to hear. At any rate, Rehoboam did not have the wisdom that his father had when he came to the throne. He made a wrong decision because he listened to the wrong counsel.

It is a basic principle in Scripture that we must start as servants before we can become rulers. This explains why David was such a success. He began as a servant—a shepherd—and proved that he could be trusted to obey orders and get the job done. Unless we are faithful over a few things, God will never trust us with many things. The person who lacks knowledge of what it means to be under authority has no right to exercise authority over others. Even our Lord Jesus Christ came to earth as God's Servant and then was exalted to the throne as the Sovereign (Phil. 2:5–11).

If Rehoboam had humbled himself and become a servant to the people, he would have saved himself and his nation a great deal of tragedy and sorrow. The wise elders gave him the secret of success: serve the people for their good, listen to them, answer them compassionately, and encourage them (12:7).

The Africans have a proverb, "The chief is servant of all." Jesus said the same thing to his disciples when they were wrangling over who was the greatest in the kingdom: "...whoever desires to become great among you, let him be your servant. And whoever desires to be first among you, let him be your slave" (Matt. 20:26–27). Our modern world laughs at that philosophy, just as the Roman world laughed in Jesus' day; but the principle still holds true. If we are going to lead for the good of others and the glory of God, we must first be servants.

Rehoboam certainly missed his opportunity for greatness. Instead of using his authority to help his subjects, he used the people to build his authority. He did not identify with their problems and pains. So long as he had what he wanted, that was really all that mattered. There is a word for it—selfishness.

Paul wrote that church officers are to *use* their offices and not just *fill* them (1 Tim. 3:13). How should we use them? By serving God's people. We must be servants who lead and leaders who serve. As we seek to serve God and his people, we must be careful to listen to them and share their burdens. We must speak encouragingly to them and help them along the way. They are not here to serve us—we are here to serve them.

After all, if the Son of God was willing to become a Servant on our behalf, could there be any higher calling than to follow in his steps? A Christian is never more like the Lord Jesus Christ than when he is sacrificially serving others.

4

Ask the Right Questions!
Nehemiah 1–2:8

We are not surprised at Nehemiah's concern over the conditions of God's people in Jerusalem. After all, he was a Jew, even though he was in Babylon! Nehemiah wanted to help, but it took four months for him to get started. Eventually God used him to guide the rebuilding of the walls, although it must have been hard to wait those four months.

We never like living with unmet needs or unresolved problems. We want closure, the sooner the better! Of course, meeting needs is important, and so is solving problems. But before jumping into the process of problem solving, we need to answer some important questions. With Nehemiah as our guide, we can discover both the right questions to ask and the right order in which to ask them:

1. *Has God made us aware of this need?* We are not prepared for Nehemiah's response to the news from Jerusalem—he weeps and mourns, fasts and prays—for a long time (1:4). His concern and distress over the people and the city were great. There was a burden on his heart, placed there by God.

Nehemiah did not immediately begin making plans to rebuild the walls of Jerusalem. For four

19

months (1:1–2:1), he did his job for the king, and he prayed and waited on God. Over that period of time, Nehemiah knew that the burden was from God and that he should act on it. We must likewise be careful that our "burdens" are really from God.

Too often, when a need arises, the first question is "How much will it cost?" In fact, when Jesus was preparing to feed the five thousand, Philip's first response was financial: "Two hundred denarii worth of bread is not sufficient..." (John 6:7). Like most of us, he began with human resources, instead of with God. First we must confirm that God is at work. Then we can move ahead. We must not waste time on projects God has not ordained for us! If God has made us aware of a need, he will use it as an opportunity to teach and bless us.

2. *What does God want us to do?* The predictably human responses to discovering a problem are calling meetings, gathering resources, and passing resolutions. Philip took a survey on the feasibility of feeding the crowd; Andrew found a boy with a lunch, but he remained skeptical about the chances of a meal for "so many" (John 6:7–9).

Nehemiah's response to the need to rebuild walls was to pray, fast, and wait for God's leading (1:4). God's purposes are not always immediately obvious. The four months of waiting were used to prepare the heart of the king (2:4–8). If Nehemiah had been impulsive in acting, the walls might never have been rebuilt!

Before we take steps we cannot retrace, we should take some spiritual action. Pray about the need and give God time to answer. Time spent waiting for God is never wasted, especially if used to plan what might be needed. Nehemiah invested the four months in thinking through what materials and human resources he would require. When the king asked, "What do you request?" (2:4), Nehemiah "prayed to the God of heaven" and told the king exactly what was needed and how long it would take! He knew that "the good hand" of his God was upon him (v. 8).

3. *Are we trusting God to provide?* All too often we limit meeting needs to the current amount in the church treasury. If the cost of the need and the balance at the bank do not agree, the need goes unmet!

Nehemiah did not start with the matter of human resources. He began with the God of unlimited resources. He knew that since God had burdened him to rebuild Jerusalem's walls, God was also responsible for providing the needed wherewithall. Nehemiah prayed, and God opened the king's heart to supply generously what was required.

"Faith is living without scheming," someone once said. If we are busy pulling strings and manipulating people to find resources, we are probably not trusting God to provide. Of course, we should use our minds to discover and utilize wisely the resources God gives us. We must also believe that if the work is of God, we can let him know our needs and trust him to act. It may well be that God is calling you to take a step of faith today. Have you got the courage?

Needs and problems will keep on confronting us in our personal lives and as church leaders. Let us respond to them in the right way—with prayer, patience, and planning. And don't forget to ask the right questions!

21

5

While Under Construction
Nehemiah 2:9–20

A man who had finally survived the process of having a house built proposed these axioms of new-home construction:

Expect it to cost more than you expected.

Expect it to take longer than you expected.

Expect it to be different from what you expected.

Expect to live with the results.

The process of building is never trouble-free. Just as people still build houses, Christians still build churches—both the physical structure and the spiritual body that meets in the building.

Nehemiah and the people of Jerusalem rebuilt the city's walls, and there are lessons we should learn from their experience. As church leaders, we are building a ministry, and the construction process did not end once the building program was completed. We are always in the process of erecting a spiritual temple. As we seek to construct (or "remodel") a spiritual ministry, what lessons do we need to learn?

Building takes preparation. Before one brick was laid, Nehemiah inspected the entire ruined wall so as to learn the situation firsthand (2:12–15). He wanted to form a workable strategy that would accomplish the task in the most efficient way.

Notice the steps Nehemiah took as he formulated the plan for rebuilding the walls. First, he sought God's guidance (v. 12). Just as God had brought him from Susa to Jerusalem with the king's permission to appropriate materials (vv. 7–9), so God would also provide wisdom for doing the work. Next, Nehemiah got all the facts. Certainly he listened to the local leaders, but he also saw the city for himself. His plan of action was based on facts, not speculation. Nehemiah also exercised patience, waiting three days before initiating activity (v. 11). Nothing is accomplished by running ahead of God. Finally, he developed an approach to the people that would win their support. After all, *they* were going to do the work. Neither spiritual growth nor the expansion of a ministry just happens—we have to plan for it. Nehemiah's thorough preparation paved the way for success.

Building takes cooperation. Nehemiah, the leaders, and the people had to work in concert to rebuild the walls. Nehemiah was quick to identify himself with the people and the city of Jerusalem. In verse 17, he addresses the people by using the terms "we" and "us." Their needs were also his, and that shared sense of need bound them together. Those who lead today need to communicate that same sense of identity with the people they serve.

They shared together a common goal: rebuild the walls! Everyone in Jerusalem knew the importance of a strong wall. It meant protection from enemies and was a step toward reestablishing their identity as God's people, separate from the world. It was the thought of reaching their goal and ending their "reproach" that motivated them. Nehemiah did not have to "buy" cooperation—it came from people committed to an important cause that they recognized as such.

Under God, Nehemiah provided leadership, and the people followed. When trusted leaders follow the Lord, the people will follow the leaders. Nehemiah earned their confidence, and so must leaders in today's church. Almost everyone contributed to rebuilding the wall (Neh. 3), and the job was done in fifty-two days of working together.

Building invites opposition. This is another lesson we must grasp. As the walls went up, the enemy showed up to mock and disrupt the work (v. 19). Although they accused Nehemiah of being a traitor to the king, Nehemiah affirmed his trust in God and kept laying bricks (v. 20).

You can count on it—as soon as God's people begin to accomplish a good work, opposition always comes in one way or another. Jesus was baptized, and Satan came to tempt him. Paul and Silas took the gospel to Philippi, and they ended up in jail. The new walls enclosing Jerusalem created a distinction between God's people and their neighbors. The neighbors did not like being "outsiders," so they caused trouble. When anyone begins to exert a spiritual influence for good, there will always be some response by the forces of evil.

Sad to say, sometimes the opposition comes from inside a group. Paul constantly had to defend his ministry against the Judaizers, other Christians who sought to tear down what the apostle achieved for Christ. Whenever a church board approves a new direction for ministry, someone in the fellowship will probably blast it. Satan works in our midst, as well as from the outside.

When opposition comes, we must respond as Nehemiah did: reaffirm that God called us to the task and will give us success (v. 20). Nehemiah knew the people were weak and vulnerable, but he also knew God's strength would see them through. Despite the enemy's interference, the wall was completed!

We are building a ministry for God. He will guide us as we plan. If we work together toward our goal and do not run from opposition, we will keep building—by God's grace.

6
How to Help
Texts from Job

The telephone rings. You pick it up and hear a tale of tragedy about someone you know. You put the telephone down and ask yourself, "What do I do now?" Few of us are professional counselors or doctors. We want to help, but we don't want to be shallow or trite—or do the *wrong* thing.

While church programs are important and the daily business must be done, we are really dealing with people's needs in all we do. Many of the people we come into contact with are hurting. They come with burdens, and we need to lighten the load.

Job suffered as few people have. We know his story. His friends came to sit with him and wanted to help him. Some things they did well; others they failed at miserably. With Job's friends as our models, we can discover four positive responses to use when we are called upon to help.

Caring. When Job's friends heard of his calamity, they came to be with him (2:11–13). They were so overwhelmed by what they found that they sat in silence for a week! But they did *come.* Our first response, like theirs, must be showing that we care. It may not seem like much, but simply being there with someone who hurts does help. Sometimes this is called "the ministry of presence." Just by sitting with those who suffer, listening to them talk, holding their hand, even providing a handkerchief, can accomplish more than any words.

Christians "weep with those who weep" (Rom. 12:15) because our tears show we care. Job's friends wept over him (2:12). They stayed with him for a week, trying to understand, offering their sympathy and concern, just by being there. As we begin to minister to those in need, we must show that we do care.

Listening. After the week of silence ended, Job began to speak (Job 3). Although his words were not surprising, given all he had been through, his friends were shocked. Job said he wished he had never been born (v. 3), that he wished he were dead (vv. 20–21), and he blamed God for what had happened (v. 23). His friends heard and reacted to Job's words, but they would have done better had they listened more carefully. That is a second helpful response— to listen.

You see, his friends heard the *words* Job said, but they did not feel the *pain* that caused those words. Instead, they argued with him! (Chapters 3 through 37 consist of one continuous argument.) A good listener responds to feelings, not so much to the words themselves. A perceptive listener discovers the meanings behind or beneath the words. People who hurt need to talk, but they require a sympathetic listener who tries to understand their pain.

Job's friends turned his suffering into a theological debate. That cheapened his experience, making him a "case" to be studied instead of a *person* to be affirmed. To minister to someone in need, we must use both ears and only a few words.

Accepting. The third response that helps to lighten the load is to accept the person and his or her words of despair. In chapter 10, Job directly accuses God of causing his trouble. While this was not the case (we know that because we can read Job 1–2, and he could not), it still *felt* to Job as if God were responsible. His friends got defensive and argued: if Job was right, their theology was all wrong. They got so intellectually involved that they ignored Job's emotional needs.

When people are in the midst of grief or pain, they say things that may shock us. There is no need for us to rush to God's defense. He can handle people being angry with him. We also do not need to explain everything; explanations do not always ease the pain. Let people question God, express their anger, vent their frustration—and still be their friend. Accepting a person does not mean agreeing with everything he or she says or does. It does mean you will be a friend, regardless. Many times sufferers have been convinced that God still loved them, just because a Christian friend stayed by their side.

Encouraging. A fourth response that helps people is to encourage them. Job called his friends "miserable comforters" (16:2) because they only made him feel worse. Our job as helpers is to offer strength and hope.

An encourager is someone who puts his or her strength at another's disposal. When a football player goes down, his teammates support him on both sides to help him walk off the field. Their strength carries him—they are encouragers. In like manner, the Holy Spirit ministers to believers by giving them the strength to go on (cf. John 14:16).

How do we offer encouragement? Emotionally, we can assure those who hurt that God loves them and that we do, too. We can share their tears and thus enter into their pain. Physically, we can do practical things—run errands, make a meal, do the laundry. Spiritually, we can pray for and with them, open God's Word, and demonstrate God's love by being loving in our own way. We also encourage by allowing them to make decisions for themselves—and offering hope.

Sometimes we see a need and want to help, but we are afraid of doing or saying the wrong thing. It is much better to do or say something than to do nothing at all. Follow these responses and ask the Spirit for wisdom. He will help us to be people who lighten the load.

7

Living on the Level
Psalm 26

If a person does not have integrity, whatever else he or she has will amount to very little in the eyes of God. It is especially important that we who are Christian leaders have integrity, the kind of character that people can trust. The opposite of integrity is duplicity, and God says that a double-minded man is "unstable in all his ways" (James 1:8). Just as an "integer" is a whole number, as opposed to a "fraction," people with integrity have wholeness. There is nothing in their lives that is divided or disloyal.

In Psalm 26, David explains the characteristics of the person who has integrity:

First, the person with integrity lives by faith in the Lord and obedience to his Word. The observation that "faith is living without scheming" is certainly true. Once we start to scheme and plot in order to get God's Word accomplished, we stop walking by faith. "I have trusted in the LORD," says David (v. 1). "...I have walked in Your truth" (v. 3).

We walk by faith when we obey the Word of God, no matter how we feel or what we see. Too often we imitate Jacob and try to "help God" accomplish his purposes by means of our own plans and skills. It took God over twenty years to teach Jacob to walk by faith and not by sight. "The Lord helps those who help themselves" is an oversimplification born out of the pits of hell. The Lord helps those who trust him, obey his Word, and yield themselves to him for whatever he wants to do.

Second, the person with integrity has nothing to hide (v. 2), because one's heart and life are an open book before God and men. When someone told Charles Haddon Spurgeon, the great British preacher, that he wanted to write his biography, Spurgeon replied, "You may write my life in the skies—I have nothing to hide!"

In verse 2, David is actually praying, "Put me to the test! Try me! Examine me!" The person with integrity is not afraid of the tests of life. Put him or her into the fiery furnace, and the result will be pure gold. Although the double-minded person falls apart when the going gets tough, the person with integrity is only made stronger.

Third, the person with integrity lives by God's love (v. 3). "Your love is ever before me" is the way the New International Version reads. Love is the divine "cement" that holds one's life together. Once selfishness gets into our hearts, we start to be double-minded and fall apart. If we cultivate our love for God and for others, we will maintain our integrity.

Fourth, when you have integrity, you hate evil and maintain high standards of personal conduct (vv. 4–5). "You who love the LORD, hate evil! ..." (Ps. 97:10). Like the man described in Psalm 1:1, David was careful where he walked and with whom he sat. It is not enough simply to love the things of the

31

Lord; we must also hate the things of the devil. Integrity is not only something we profess; it is something we practice. People can see it in our lives. If they have to ask, then we must have lost it!

People with integrity are concerned primarily about God's honor and glory (vv. 6–8). This is why they keep their hands clean, so that nothing will bring disgrace to the glorious name of the Lord. Where will you find people with integrity? At the altar, the place of sacrifice and worship. Like Abraham, they have their altar, and there they worship God and offer their very best to the Lord.

Finally, the person with integrity maintains that integrity, no matter what others may say or do (vv. 9–12). Others may sin against the Lord and be "bloodthirsty," but people with integrity will go on walking in that integrity. Others may threaten them or offer bribes, but they will follow the Lord and not yield to such enticements.

The double-minded person is "unstable in all his ways," but the person with integrity maintains stability in a slippery world: "I shall not slip" (v. 1). "My foot stands in an even place" (v. 12). The word *even* simply means "a level place." Literally, the person with integrity is "on the level"! You can trust him or her to stand firm.

When we lose our integrity, we lose our opportunity for ministry, because God cannot trust us and others will not trust us either. David looks back and says, "I have walked in my integrity" (v. 1). Then he looks ahead and vows, "I will walk in my integrity..." (v. 11). He was a man after God's own heart. No wonder God blessed him and used him!

8
Have a Good Day!
Psalm 34:11–22

Who is the man or woman who "loves life and desires to see many good days" (Ps. 34:12, NIV)? The answer to that question is: "Anybody in his right mind!" Of course, the basic problem is that people disagree over what a "good day" really is. For those of us who are Christians, "good days" involve much more than material gain or personal pleasure. There is a spiritual dimension that makes a day "good" for us and for those whose lives we touch.

It is worth noting that "good days" can even include "troubles" (v. 17), "a broken heart" (v. 18), and "afflictions" (v. 19). God does not promise to shelter us from trials, but he does promise to give us grace to bear them and faith to keep going until he brings us through. "Good days" are days that do us good, even if they bring burdens and battles.

How can you and I be sure that our days will be "good" and to the glory of God? David tells us in Psalm 34 that there are certain conditions that we must meet:

We must watch what we say (v. 13). It is amazing how much trouble we can avoid if we will only control our tongues. James tells us that the tongue

33

is like a poisonous beast and a destructive fire (James 3:5–8). Of course, if an animal is tamed and a fire is controlled, they will give you power and service; but if they are out of control, watch out!

It is the heart that controls the tongue. "...For out of the abundance of the heart the mouth speaks" (Matt. 12:34). We need to pray with the psalmist, "Set a guard, O LORD, over my mouth; Keep watch over the door of my lips. Do not incline my heart to any evil thing..." (Ps. 141:3–4).

We must determine to do good and seek peace (v. 14). While there are many things in life that we cannot control, the one thing we can control is the kingdom within, the "thoughts and intents of the heart" (Heb. 4:12). Outlook often determines outcome. If we look for good, we will find it; if we seek peace, we will discover it. But if we decide that conflict is inevitable—well, war is sure to come!

All of us have had the unfortunate experience of starting off the morning "on the wrong foot" and having a miserable day. Why was the day a failure? Because our attitudes were negative and critical. We were sensitive and touchy, and therefore nothing went right.

This is one reason why we must begin each day with the Lord and make sure our hearts are free from selfishness and anger. What we get out of the day depends largely on what we put into it. If we live by faith and in love, then God can give us a "good day."

We must seek to please the Lord in everything (vv. 15–16). If we live only to please ourselves, we will reap the sad consequences of selfishness. Of course, if we seek only to please others, they may

34

enslave us and make doormats out of us! But if we live to please the Lord, he will rule and overrule in every situation, and all things will indeed "work together for good" (Rom. 8:28).

It is comforting to know that God's eyes are always upon us. It is also an encouragement for us to walk in the right paths, in obedience to his Word. God sees us; nothing can be hidden from his eyes. It brings real freedom and joy to your life when you walk in the light of his countenance, with his smile of blessing upon you.

We must pray and keep in touch with God (v. 17). "Pray without ceasing" (1 Thess. 5:17) simply means, "Stay in constant communion with your Father in heaven." Prayer can keep us out of trouble, and prayer can take us through trouble by transforming trouble into triumph. Prayer power is the greatest force in the universe. We must begin each day with believing prayer, and we must pray throughout the day and when the day ends. When you unlock the day with the key of prayer, God's blessing will go with you.

We must humble ourselves before God (v. 18). Most of the troubles in life come because of pride, either our own or somebody else's. We all need that broken heart and contrite spirit that David prayed about (Ps. 51:17). If we "walk humbly with our God" (Mic. 6:8), all of the resources of heaven will be at our disposal. If we insist on having our own way, God will leave us to our own plans and powers, and we will fail miserably.

God still scorns and resists the proud and gives grace to the humble (Prov. 3:34; 1 Peter 5:5). Nobody who walks around acting important can expect God to give him a "good day." Pride goes before destruction and a haughty spirit before a fall (Prov. 16:18).

Humility does not mean we must think poorly of ourselves. It means that we do not concentrate on ourselves, because we are busy thinking of others and seeking to serve them in the name of Christ. Humility is not weakness; rather, it is power under control. When we walk with the Lord in meekness, he can give us "good days" for our good and his glory.

Each morning, the Father says to us, "Have a good day!" And he tells us how to do it! Will we listen and obey?

9

What Will We Leave Behind?
Psalm 78:1–8

The church of Jesus Christ is always one generation short of extinction. What we do today, both as individuals and as leaders in the church, will greatly affect our children and our grandchildren. We have a solemn obligation to them—and to the Lord—to be faithful in our witness and our work. We want the coming generations to know the glory of the Lord and the blessings that flow when we follow him.

In other words, you and I will be leaving something behind for the next generation. The important question is: *What* will that legacy be? Let us consider some of the well-known people found in the Bible to discover what they left behind. Then we can better evaluate the lasting nature of our own ministries.

Wherever Abraham and Isaac traveled, they left behind altars and wells (Gen. 13:1–4; 26:24–25). You could trace their journeys by following the altars they built and the wells they dug. The altar, of course, speaks of their worship of God; the well reminds us of God's provision for their daily needs. Jesus used water to illustrate the ministry of the Holy Spirit and the presence of God's refreshing and empowering life in the believer (John 4:13–14; 7:37–39). If other pilgrims so desired, they could use the altars and drink from the wells that Abraham and Isaac left behind as reminders for others that they must worship God and depend on him.

If we were to trace the journeys of the children of Israel, we would find their steps marked by graves. You will recall that Israel refused to believe God and enter the land that God had promised them. As a result, the nation wandered in the wilderness for forty years, while the older generation died off. It was history's longest funeral march, and each grave was a monument to the unbelief of the people. What a tragedy it would be if *our* generation were remembered only for its unbelief! How we need to trust God and obey him by faith, lest we wander around, miss his best for our ministry, and leave behind dead memorials to our unbelief.

Paul said that David "served his own generation" (Acts 13:36), but he also served the generations that followed. What was David's legacy? For one thing, he left behind songs and musical instruments for the worship of God (2 Chron. 29:25–30; Neh. 12:36). The nation of Israel was better able to praise God because of the rich musical heritage that King David left. It was David who organized the temple choirs, wrote much of the music, and even developed the instruments that the Levites played.

The worship of God is the church's most important duty and greatest privilege. Are we giving to the generation to come the equipment they need for the worship of the Lord? Or are we leaving behind cheap materials and shallow songs that fall short of glorifying God?

David also left the succeeding generations weapons of war with which to fight the enemy (2 Kings 11:10). If Satan cannot defeat our own generation, he will continue his assault on the church by attacking the next generation. Have we really prepared our children, and have they prepared our grandchildren, to meet Satan and conquer him?

It has been said that the first generation fights the battles, the second generation claims the spoils and enjoys them, and the third generation sells out to the enemy. This may not be true in every family or every ministry, but it has happened enough times to encourage us to be on our guard. Joshua's generation served the Lord, and so did the generation that followed; but that third generation started to turn away from the Lord and follow the ways of the world (Josh. 24:31; Judg. 2:6–13). We must warn the generation to come that the enemy is still active, and we must put into their hands the weapons they need to fight a winning battle—the Word of God, prayer, separation from sin, and faith in the living God.

Abraham and Isaac left behind wells and altars, yet the nation of Israel left behind thousands of graves, monuments to their unbelief. David's bequest included songs of praise, instruments of worship, and weapons of war. Judas left behind a graveyard (Matt. 27:3–10), but Jesus' gift to future generations was an empty tomb! The graveyard was a symbol of defeat, but the empty tomb represents final victory. We remember Judas as a traitor, a hypocrite who was unfaithful to the Lord. But we remember Jesus as the Faithful Servant of the Lord, obedient to the Father's will, even to the point of dying on a cross.

You and I cannot avoid leaving an inheritance for the next generation. What we leave will either help them in their Christian walk or hinder them in the journey. It will either encourage this ministry or weaken its effectiveness. The decisions that we make, the examples that we set, the spiritual work that we do—all of these will help to make up the legacy we leave for the generation to follow. And why do we want to leave a rich spiritual heritage? "That they may set their hope in God, And not forget the works of God, But keep His commandments" (Ps. 78:7).

10

Hanging Together— Or Separately?
Psalm 133

At the signing of the Declaration of Independence on July 4, 1776, Benjamin Franklin said, "We must all hang together, or assuredly we shall all hang separately." Those patriots *did* hang together, and the result was the birth of a new nation.

The theme of this Psalm of David is the unity of God's people. There is a great difference between "unity" and "uniformity," and we must take care to remember and maintain that distinction. Unity comes from the life that is within, while uniformity is the result of power and pressure from without. Uniformity is brittle and can be easily destroyed, while true unity is strong and enduring. Uniformity leaves no room for honest differences, while unity recognizes the diversity of individuals and is stronger because of it.

Three times each year, all Jewish men were expected to go to Jerusalem to celebrate the feasts— Passover, Pentecost, and Tabernacles. It was a joyful time for them as they journeyed to the holy city, and no doubt the holiday atmosphere contributed to their sense of brotherhood. They rejoiced in their unity.

But David wanted something deeper than this

occasional unity. He wanted God's people to "dwell together in unity" (v. 1). It is one thing to travel with somebody you may not like, and even get along with him or her for a week or two. But it is quite something else to live with that person all year long!

It is unfortunate when God's people cannot get along with each other. Lack of spiritual unity weakens the fellowship, grieves the Holy Spirit, and hurts the testimony of the Lord. The unsaved in the community rejoice when they hear about church "fights" or "splits," because this kind of news gives them one more excuse not to take the gospel seriously.

Let us examine David's little song and learn from it how we can promote and strengthen unity in our own fellowship and thereby bring joy to God's heart:

Remember that we are members of the same family. You might expect brothers and sisters to get along with each other—but, alas, too often they do not! The first murder recorded in biblical history involved two brothers, when Cain killed Abel. Moses had problems with his brother and sister, Aaron and Miriam. Joseph was hated by his brothers and sold for a slave.

Those who have been born again by the Spirit of God belong to the same family, the family of God. We can call God our Father and think of all other true believers as our brothers and sisters in Christ. We share the same divine nature and are headed for the same heavenly home. While we may have our disagreements and differences, the things we have in common far outweigh them all.

Remember that spiritual unity comes down from God. This is not something that we ourselves "work up" or manufacture. It is not too difficult to establish uniformity, but true unity must come from within and from above. It is a spiritual miracle.

David uses two illustrations in Psalm 133 to get this point across. The first has to do with the anointing of the high priest with the special oil (v. 2; cf. Exod. 29:1–7). The oil is a symbol of the Spirit of God, who has been poured out upon God's people. David makes it clear that this oil ran down Aaron's beard, so from there it must have run to the ephod which Aaron wore over his heart. On the ephod were twelve stones, one for each tribe of Israel (Exod. 28:4–12). In other words, the oil bathed those twelve separate stones and united them as one. They did not lose their individual distinctiveness but were simply united by the oil of anointment.

So it is when we allow the Holy Spirit to control our lives. He brings us together in a deep spiritual unity. We do not lose our own individual personalities, as so often happens with imposed uniformity. Rather, our purpose becomes one in heart, mind, and spirit.

The second illustration, in verse 3, comes from the world of weather: the dew falls on the ground and brings life to the vegetation. Mount Hermon is over nine thousand feet high, and the dew that falls from Mount Hermon is like rain! This dew brings life to the fields, and the result is both beauty and fruitfulness.

Neither the oil nor the dew is noisy, for they symbolize the Holy Spirit as he graciously works among God's people. Both the oil and the dew come down, because they are sent of God. Spiritual unity is not attained by special meetings or fervent activi-

43

ties. True unity comes quietly when we allow the Spirit of the Lord to work in our lives.

Remember that spiritual unity is practical. Unity is good, like the dew, and it is pleasant, like the anointing oil. We desire unity in the Lord, not so that we can selfishly enjoy it, but so that we can better serve the Lord. When a church has spiritual unity, there is a fragrance and a clearly seen fruitfulness—to the glory of God.

Where does God send his blessing? "...there the LORD commanded the blessing..." (v. 3). Where? Wherever he saw the dew and the oil! If the oil of the Spirit and the dew of the Spirit are upon our lives and our ministries, then God's blessing will surely follow.

As an encouragement to our own unity, let us read this little psalm together and take it to heart. "Behold, how good and how pleasant it is for brethren to dwell together in unity!"

11
Praise Changes Things!
Psalm 147:1–6

Psalm 147 begins and ends with "Praise the LORD!" and this is good counsel for us to follow. We are too prone to take God's mercies for granted, to forget the wonderful benefits that come to our lives when we sincerely praise the Lord. Of course, we are not to praise the Lord *because* of what we will get out of it! We praise him because he is worthy of our praise, and because worship and praise are the highest activities of the Christian believer.

But the Christian who is faithful to praise the Lord does experience certain blessings that can come no other way. This psalm describes those blessings for us and, in so doing, encourages us in our praise of God.

Praise makes life beautiful (v. 1). Praise is both "good" and "pleasant," and it is also "beautiful." We need never ask, "Is this a good time to praise the Lord?" It is *always* a good time to praise the Lord! There are times when it is improper to debate or to laugh or perhaps even to smile, but all times are the right times for praising the Lord.

Praise adds those extra spiritual ingredients that help make our lives beautiful. The person who does not praise God is often self-centered, critical, and proud—and there is very little beauty in that kind of life. "Worship the LORD in the beauty of holiness" (Ps. 29:2b).

Praise builds our lives (v. 2a). Criticizing and complaining always tear down God's work. It takes very little effort to find fault with each other and with the church, but it requires a good deal of grace to praise God when things may not please us. When you and I sincerely praise the Lord, the Holy Spirit builds our lives and helps us to accomplish his work.

Whenever there is revival in the church, it usually brings a new emphasis on praise. Why? Because God builds his work through worship. It is not enough for us to study the Bible, pray, and give of our time and money. We must also give of ourselves in praise to the Lord. When we do, God puts all of our devotional exercises together and builds us spiritually.

Praise unites God's people (v. 2b). Jewish men were required to go to Jerusalem to celebrate the feasts—Passover, Pentecost, and Tabernacles. These were times of great national unity as they forgot their personal and tribal differences and assembled to praise the Lord. Perhaps this explains why there is so much praise recorded in the Book of Revelation. When God's people gather in glory, we will be united in worship and in praise. Here and now we may be divided over explaining the Bible or our methods of ministry, but one thing we all agree on is praising the Lord. Just think of how many different denominations are represented in a Christian hymnal!

46

The next time we find ourselves disagreeing and dividing, it might be a good idea just to stop and praise the Lord. People who pray together, stay together— and people who sing together, cling together!

Praise heals the wounds (vv. 3–4). We must never forget that the church is here to minister to wounded lives and broken hearts. There are many who need spiritual healing, and praise is a part of that medicine. Paul and Silas in prison sang praises to God, not only as a witness to the other prisoners, but also as a balm of healing for their own lives. When we are hurt, Satan likes to infect our wounds with the poisons of malice and bitterness, but praise to God will immediately disinfect those wounds, no matter how deep they may be.

It seems incredible that the God of the galaxies, the God who knows the number and the names of the stars (v. 4) is concerned about our broken hearts! "Casting all your care upon Him, for he cares for you" (1 Peter 5:7).

Praise releases power (v. 5a). The modern church is just beginning to discover the power of praise, but the Old Testament Jews knew that power firsthand. As the nation of Israel marched through the wilderness, they praised the Lord and carried the ark of the covenant before them (Num. 10:33–36). The psalms reflect Israel's faith in God and in his power to see them through. When David was discouraged, he often picked up his harp and sang praise to God, and then everything started to change for the better.

Yes, there is power in praise, when that praise comes from a heart that loves Christ and trusts him. There is also power in complaining and murmuring—but it is power to tear down, not for building.

47

Praise makes us teachable (v. 5b). "His understanding is infinite," and we could never begin to comprehend all that God is and does and says. But, as we praise him, our hearts and minds are better prepared to understand him. The church's worship before the preaching of the Word is not only our expression of praise, but it is also our preparation of heart. Because we sincerely worship God, we can better understand his truth and his will for our lives.

Praise lifts us up and helps us to win our battles (v. 6). Praise is a mighty weapon against the powers of darkness! Satan is the accuser (Rev. 12:10), and he hates it when God's people worship the Father. He would much rather we spend our time finding things to criticize and complain about.

The fact that praise lifts us up and brings encouragement is not due to some psychological trick. It is the work of the Holy Spirit, who is the very Spirit of praise (Eph. 5:18ff). When we truly praise the Lord, we lay hold of the power of his throne of grace, and he is able to work in us and through us to accomplish his purposes.

"Praise the LORD! For it is good to sing praises to our God...." And praise makes a difference!

12
Weigh Your Words
Texts from Proverbs

Jesus warned that one day we will give an account for the words we have used (Matt. 12:36). Just stop and think of all the words you have used in conversations today! It should make you realize how important it is to use words carefully. As we conduct our business here, we will use a lot of words. Let us look to some verses in the Book of Proverbs to discover the importance of weighing our words, so that we will not be careless in speaking.

Our words reveal our character. Proverbs 10:11 (NASB) reads: "The mouth of the righteous is a fountain of life, But the mouth of the wicked conceals violence." To put this briefly, what we say announces to people what we are really like.

If you listen to the vocabulary a person uses, you can often tell what his or her vocation is. A mechanic will talk about torque converters and spark-plug gaps. Bankers mention rates of interest, certificates of deposit, and foreclosures. Crankbaits, surface lures, line strength, and spinning reels are terms that sprinkle the speech of fishermen. Similarly, when people hear us speak, they can tell if we love

Christ, if we care about others, if we are kind—they can even tell what our priorities are!

Jesus said, "…the mouth speaks out of that which fills the heart" (Matt. 12:34, NASB). The heart is where character is forged, and that is what motivates our words. This is why we need to be nourished on the Word of God, spend time in prayer, and seek the guidance of the Holy Spirit. Then our character will be godly, and our words will reflect it. Our words are worth only as much as our character!

Our words have consequences. "There is one who speaks rashly like the thrusts of a sword, But the tongue of the wise brings healing" (Prov. 12:18 NASB). This verse presents a second reason to weigh our words. When a man first says to a woman, "I love you," a process begins. Often the man then proves his love by purchasing a diamond ring, a symbol that one day they will stand before God to exchange wedding vows. All this was caused by saying those three simple words: "I love you."

Proverbs 12:18 tells us that words are powerful. They have the power to cut and wound, but they also have the power to heal. Words spoken in anger and unkindness can cause problems for a lifetime. A soft answer to angry words can bring good out of evil and win a friend. In a sense, words are like seeds—once they are sown, they inevitably produce a harvest. The words we say today as we transact our business are going to have consequences. Let us use words in such a way that they produce a harvest of peace and joy!

Our words are measured by our conduct. Proverbs 26:24–25 introduces us to a man who speaks beautiful words, but they only disguise evil inten-

50

tions: "He who hates disguises it with his lips, but he lays up deceit in his heart. When he speaks graciously, do not believe him..." (NASB). Our words and actions have to be consistent; otherwise our words will make us liars—"And a flattering mouth works ruin" (v. 28b, NASB).

Parents sometimes say to their children, "Do as I say, not as I do!" But what we do often carries more weight than anything we say. If we profess to love and follow Christ but do not back up our words with our behavior, we cannot blame folks for being suspicious, can we?

A word of caution: our words must never be a substitute for action. James 2:15–17 instructs us to prove our faith not just by the words we use, but by the things we do.

It may be that before we get down to the business of the church, there are some important words that need to be said. Words like "I apologize; I was wrong." Or "You're a blessing to me." Or just the simple politeness of "Please" and "Thank you."

We have to use words to communicate. Be sure you weigh them first!

13
Rocks, Rivers, and Righteousness
Isaiah 32:1–2

If you have visited a bookstore lately, then you know that "leadership" is a popular theme for books and magazine articles. In this competitive world, people want to know how to get to the top as quickly and easily as possible. Everybody seems to be looking for that secret of effective leadership that will guarantee success.

But what is a successful leader? What are his or her characteristics? Does God have the same view of leadership as that promoted by big business or government? Can a person be a successful leader in business and not be successful when it comes to the work of the Lord?

These two verses from Isaiah picture God's ideal leader. No doubt they are descriptive of our Lord Jesus Christ, the great "Rock of Ages" who was smitten for us. We know that one day he will "reign in righteousness," and all who have trusted him will enjoy the blessings of that reign. But these verses also describe the kind of leaders God is looking for in his work today.

The prophet uses two different pictures to describe God's ideal leader—a rock and a river. What is there about a rock and a river that we should know so that we might become better leaders in the work God has given us to do?

Balance. For one thing, in these two images you see balance. A rock changes very slowly, but a river is constantly changing. A great rock does not move, but a river is ever flowing. You have to go around the rock, but a river is very adaptable and cuts its own course.

The leader who is like the rock is admired for his strength and stability. His theme song is "I shall not be moved!" But there are times when even the most dedicated leader must be like the river and make room for change, times when it is spiritual to adapt to new situations. If we are to be godly leaders, we must know when to stand like the rock, but also when to change like the river. God's work on earth is built on a rock of unchanging truth, and that truth must never be compromised. But God's work must constantly be manifested in new challenges and changing situations. We need leaders who are both rocks and rivers, dependable and adaptable.

Ministry. The rock and the river speak not only of balance, but also of ministry and service. The rock provides shade from the hot desert sun, and the river provides satisfaction to the thirsty traveler. Godly leaders think of what they can do for others, not what they can do for themselves. God's people have a right to look to their leaders and expect them to serve their needs, to the glory of God.

Security and satisfaction. The church is a fellowship of people who need a sense of stability and comfort from the Lord. God wants to use us, his

53

servants, to be rocks of security in a world that is filled with danger. God wants his rivers of living water to flow through us and bring life and strength to all his people (John 7:37–39). It is a solemn thing to be one of God's workers in his church. We must take care that we are truly rocks, not shifting sand dunes, and that the water of life has free course in and through us.

Challenge. Finally, these two images, the rock and the river, remind us of our calling. Like the rock, we face the challenge of standing firm for the faith and not becoming "rolling stones" that stand for nothing. But, like the river, we must move forward and cut new channels where needed. The difficult task of leadership is right there—knowing when to stand and when to move.

If Isaiah teaches us anything about leadership, he teaches us that good leadership is not a matter of "either/or" but "both/and." Some of us find it easier to be rocks, and perhaps we even boast about our unwillingness to change. Others of us are more like the river, always on the move, not afraid to change course, ready for a new challenge. God wants us to be both, and we must be both if we are to do the righteous work God has called us to do.

14
Essentials for True Ministry
Isaiah 50:4–7

You cannot read these verses in Isaiah without seeing in them a picture of our Lord Jesus Christ, God's Suffering Servant. Our salvation is not dependent on our following his example of perfect sacrifice, but on trusting him and the work he did for us on the cross. However, in our service for the Lord, we can find encouragement and strength as we meditate on Christ's example as the Servant of God.

Let us notice several essentials for ministry that are revealed in the life and service of Jesus Christ.

An open ear (vv. 4a–5). The image here is that of a servant, rising early in the morning to receive his master's orders. Jesus arose very early in the morning and went out to a solitary place to pray (Mark 1:35). We get the impression that this was his usual practice—that he opened each day in fellowship with the Father.

How important it is for each of us to begin every day with the Lord! We can never serve him acceptably unless we spend time alone with him, listening to his Word, praying, and worshiping him. A disciplined devotional life is essential for spiritual leadership. The psalmist said, "I rise before dawn and

55

cry for help; I have put my hope in your word"
(Ps. 119:147, NIV).

If the perfect Son of God had to take time to meet with the Father, how much more do you and I need that daily "quiet time"?

A ready tongue (v. 4a). The "tongue of the learned" means an "instructed" tongue, one that knows what to say. Of course, what the tongue says comes from the heart (Matt. 12:35), so the source of a learned tongue is an instructed heart, one that readily receives the Word of God.

We never know when we will be called upon to give counsel or direction to others, and we must be ready. In our business meetings as church leaders, we must be careful to share the "wisdom that is from above" (James 3:17) and not the wisdom of the world. If we walk "in the counsel of the ungodly," we will soon be standing with sinners and sitting with the scornful (Ps. 1:1).

James reminds us (3:1–12) that the tongue is a small member of the body, but it carries a great deal of power. It can be a fire that destroys or a fire that releases warmth and power. It is like a bit and bridle on a horse, or a rudder on a ship—it helps to steer things in either the right or the wrong direction. We must take care that the words we speak do not get us on a dangerous detour.

A surrendered will (5b–6a). The picture here is not a very pretty one, for we see Jesus giving his body to be abused by his captors. It was for us that he was scourged, and it was for us that he was humiliated and hurt. How we ought to bow in love and worship as we contemplate what the Lord willingly endured for us!

56

Jesus' body was totally yielded to the Father because his will was totally yielded. Yes, though it meant suffering and shame, he bore it willingly. "I delight to do Your will, O my God..." (Ps. 40:8). It is not likely that you and I will be called upon to bare our backs to the lash, but we ought to have that kind of surrender and obedience in our hearts.

There is a price to pay for godly leadership. People may not scourge us with whips; they may use their tongues instead! If we are surrendered to the Lord, such suffering will not stop us from serving. As leaders in his church, we must be "steadfast, unmovable, always abounding in the work of the Lord..." (1 Cor. 15:58).

A set face (v. 7). The Lord "steadfastly set His face to go to Jerusalem" (Luke 9:51). Think of what was waiting for Jesus there—rejection, arrest, shame, suffering, death on a cross! You and I probably would have thought up several reasons for *not* going to Jerusalem, yet Jesus set his face "like flint" and obeyed the Father's will.

Dedication and determination are inseparable. There are all kinds of subtle forces that would seek to move us from the course God has set for us. Once we have discovered the Father's will, we must do it, no matter what others say or do.

When we have these characteristics, we can be sure that the Lord will help our ministry and that we will not be ashamed (v. 7). Why? Because the more we are like Jesus Christ, the easier it is for the Father to bless us and use us for his glory!

15
The Spirit of the Law
Matthew 18:15–17

Church discipline is a touchy issue, and it grows increasingly sensitive when it has to be administered. That is why we seek to prevent certain kinds of sticky situations from arising. But Jesus knew that disciplinary occasions would arise in the church, so he gave us guidelines for resolving them. Where an offense occurs, it must first be dealt with privately. If the matter remains unresolved, witnesses must be called in. The final step, if needed, is to take the matter before the church body.

Jesus gave these guidelines because he expected church leaders to resolve church problems. But there is a danger in using this passage merely as a pat formula. Consider this flawed scenario: "I went to him personally, and he didn't listen. I took witnesses, and nothing was done. Now the whole church knows. I followed the biblical guidelines—out he goes!" We are bound to obey Jesus, but we must also be in tune with the *spirit* of his words. He balanced the letter of the law with the spirit of the law—we must do the same.

There are some significant questions, based on these verses, that we can ask to help us understand the spirit of Jesus' words.

How do we treat a Christian who sins? This should be the first question. Twice in verse 15 Jesus uses the word *brother.* So we know we are to treat a believer who sins as a fellow-Christian, not as an outsider.

When someone hurts us, we tend to erect barriers and fence that person out of our lives. We arrange our schedule so we will not see that person or have to speak to him or her. But Jesus is saying that we cannot reject that person—we are both part of the same family of God. Sin grieves God, but he still loves the sinner. Sin may hurt us, but we are still spiritually related to the one who sinned.

That another Christian has sinned should never make us feel self-satisfied and superior—and certainly not happy. It grieves the Holy Spirit and should make us concerned for the individual's spiritual condition. The sin should not become a topic of conversation, either. Jesus told us to see the sinner in private, "between you and him alone" (v. 15).

Galatians 6:1 directs that "if a man is overtaken in any trespass, you who are spiritual restore such a one in a spirit of gentleness...." The "spirit of gentleness" does not mean we do not care about correcting the wrong—we do. But it means we are to treat the person who has done wrong like a brother, with respect and kindness. Sinners are not "the enemy," and we are not out to get them!

What is our goal in disciplining? If we are going to follow Christ's instruction, our aim must be to "gain" our brother (v. 15). Jesus is telling us that restoring a relationship is far more important than winning an argument. Sad to say, some Christians would rather win the argument than heal the wound.

The Pharisees were like that. It was more important to them to avoid work on the Sabbath than heal a sick man (Mark 3:1–6). The desire to "follow the rules" and then get even is neither spiritual nor biblical. Taking vengeance is *God's* prerogative (Rom. 12:19).

Our personal sense of hurt makes it difficult to think about what the person who hurt us is feeling. If the relationship is valuable to us, we must try to set things right. Perhaps it was a simple misunderstanding. "But *I* was right!" we want to say. Although we want everyone to know where the fault lies, we must remember that relationships are more important than our "rights."

One more factor to consider here is that God has certainly been patient with our sins and allowed us to experience his grace often. Since we have sinned, too, we cannot pretend to be so righteous, can we? In seeking to win a brother or sister who has wronged us or the church, bear in mind that all of us are in need of forgiveness and restoration. A humble attitude as we counsel will speed the healing process.

Do we take unity seriously? In verses 16 and 17, Jesus instructs us to include "witnesses" and then the entire church family. But the purpose is not to spread the news of the sin! If we are just following a formula, other people become judges. The spirit of Jesus' words, though, makes the witnesses and church family become loving persuaders, ready to bring about repentance and restoration.

We must be "diligent to preserve the unity of the

Spirit in the bond of peace" (Eph. 4:3, NASB). When two believers are divided, it affects the whole church. A wound needs immediate attention, or else it will fester and the poison will spread. Leaders in a church family have a great responsibility to maintain harmony. Jesus instructed us to take a problem to larger groups only to bring about healing. Only if the offender refuses to repent should he or she be removed. And even then, the removal is to preserve the oneness of Christ's church. If later there is repentance, forgiving restoration must follow (2 Cor. 2:6–8).

Any time a divisive problem surfaces, things get tense within the group. We must be sure that throughout the process of healing, our motive is *love*. The fruit of the Spirit is love, which covers a multitude of sins and strengthens the bonds of fellowship.

Sin in any relationship, including the church family, is serious. It has to be dealt with by following the pattern established by Christ. But, as we follow that pattern, we also need to be guided by his Spirit, and the spirit of his words.

16

What It Means to Be Great
Mark 10:35–45

The word *great* is overused. The world at large uses it excessively, but so does the church: "great sermon," "great preacher," "great Sunday school," "great missions program," "great church"! But what does it really mean to be "great" in Christ's service? And how do we measure this greatness?

James and John wanted to be assured of important positions when Christ established his kingdom. So they boldly requested that they be seated on either side of Jesus' throne. The Lord told them that such recognition was not available upon request: thrones were reserved for certain individuals.

When the other disciples discovered what James and John had been up to, they were upset (probably because they had not thought of it first!). Jesus took advantage of the moment to instruct his disciples on the nature of greatness in God's kingdom. Church leaders especially need to absorb this teaching. There is nothing wrong with wanting our church or organization to be great for God, provided we understand what true greatness is. Try to grasp the three principles Jesus presented about greatness in Mark 10.

1. *Greatness comes by serving* (vv. 42–44). The world's standard is the opposite: the more people

you oversee, the more authority you wield, the more salary you earn, the more influence you exercise—the "greater" you are. But to Jesus, greatness comes by stooping to serve.

Throughout the Scriptures, it is God's pattern to train leaders by first making them servants. Moses tended sheep in the desert forty years before liberating Israel. David, too, was a shepherd before he was a king. Joseph was a slave and prisoner before becoming prime minister of Egypt. The process of maturing *under* authority prepares us to be *in* authority.

Jesus put a premium on serving, not on being served. Serving builds character and instills certain qualities God wants in his leaders—humility, obedience, submission, trust. When God finds a man or woman he can trust, he has a tool he can use in powerful ways.

2. *Greatness involves sacrifice* (vv. 38–40). James and John thought they would take a shortcut to their thrones—just maneuver for them. But this did not work. After they had made their request, Jesus asked, "Can you drink the cup I drink and share the baptism I must undergo?" The cup and baptism represent the cross! James and John did not understand the cost of being on a throne, even though they *said* they were able (v. 39).

Again, this is a principle illustrated throughout the Bible. For Moses to become the leader of Israel, he had to give up the "treasures in Egypt" (Heb. 11:26). To become God's man, he had to forsake a worldly throne. Some may call it folly, but God calls it great.

Satan tempted Jesus to take his throne the easy

way: "Just bow down and worship me, and all the kingdoms of the world are yours" (*see* Matt. 4:9). Here was a crown without a cross—the easy way to greatness. But Christ refused. Because he endured the cross, God exalted him with the name "above every name" (Phil. 2:8–11). In God's kingdom, the process of suffering and sacrifice produces mature men and women who can do great things for God.

3. *Greatness is always measured by Christ* (vv. 42–45). This principle has two applications. First, Jesus is the standard by which we measure greatness; second, only Christ can determine who is truly "great" in his kingdom.

Jesus pointed to himself as an example of what he meant about service and sacrifice: "For even the Son of Man did not come to be served, but to serve, and to give His life a ransom for many" (v. 45). If you want to see how great you are, compare yourself to Christ. Of course, none of us measures up to the Lord's stature yet, but the exercise is still valuable. Take a brief inventory. Do you have Christ's patience with people? Do you trust the Father's timetable? Are you sensitive to people's needs? Do you have a kind word for someone who is hurt, wise counsel for someone who is seeking? Is God's glory your highest motivation? It is easy to compare ourselves with another Christian or church, and decide that we look good. But when we measure ourselves by Christ, we realize we have not arrived. And that should motivate us to press on!

Only Christ knows who is truly great. We tend to see the people on the platform, hear the music, listen to the radio programs, read the books—and conclude that visibility and popularity are the path to greatness. It's not necessarily so! D. L. Moody felt that much of his ministry's power came from two women who prayed faithfully for him. We know about Moody's greatness but these women were also great.

Since you must let Christ measure your life, don't grow discouraged with yourself or your ministry. He knows what you do, the sacrifices you make. Proverbs 22:29 says: "Do you see a man skilled in his work? He will stand before kings; He will not stand before obscure men" (NASB). If we are faithful in our duty, one day we will stand before the King of kings—and we will discover who the true "greats" are.

Apply these principles to your church or business. Do you sincerely seek to serve others, for Jesus' sake? When you have to make a sacrifice, do you do it willingly? Are you seeking Christ's approval, or trying to win approval from somewhere else? Be careful in using the word *great*. Because something is big, flashy, or "successful" by man's standard, does not mean that God is impressed. Give that word the content Jesus did: greatness has to do with service and sacrifice, as measured by Christ.

17
Time to Take Inventory
Luke 7:1–10

It was Socrates who said that the unexamined life was not worth living. If honest examination is important for philosophers, how much more important it is for us as believers in Christ, and especially for those who are leaders in his church! We must periodically take time to measure ourselves and our work to make sure we are all that we ought to be.

Of course, the ultimate standard is Jesus Christ our Lord, and he must always be the perfect example for us to follow (Eph. 4:13). But sometimes it does us good to look at other men and women in the Bible to see how we measure up. Luke 7:1–10 provides one such example. This Roman centurion was especially commended by Jesus Christ. What qualities in this man should we admire and, with God's help, seek to develop in our own personal lives?

Caring concern. For one thing, the centurion was a man with great concern for others. He also had a concern for the Jewish community and had helped the people build a synagogue (v. 5). This act was especially unusual because the man was a Roman, and the Romans had a tendency to look down upon the Jews and their "exclusive" religion.

It is easy for us today to judge the man's motives and suggest that he was merely buying cooperation from the Jewish leaders. But I prefer to give him the benefit of the doubt. I believe he had a personal concern for the Jewish nation and wanted to help them.

Our most important task as church leaders is to help build the church of Jesus Christ in this world. But as we do this, let us not forget that we also have obligations to our fellowman, no matter what faith an individual might profess. We are a part of the human community, and we must do our share to help others, to the glory of God. Jesus instructed us to let our light shine by doing good works (Matt. 5:16), and Paul admonished us "do good to all, especially to those who are of the household of faith" (Gal. 6:10).

This centurion also had a concern for his dying servant, although most Roman soldiers, especially officers, were somewhat hardened to death. So why would a Roman officer worry about the death of a mere slave? There were some sixty million slaves in the Roman Empire, and it would not be too difficult to replace the boy. But this servant was "dear to him" (v. 2), so much so that the centurion sent word to Jesus to come and heal the lad.

Are we leaders who show concern? Do we have a personal interest in the needs of others? Do we ever sacrifice for others? Do we intercede with the Lord on their behalf? If a pagan Roman centurion had a heart of concern for others, how much more concern should we show—we who have been saved by Christ and have experienced his love!

Humility. We note a second fine quality about this man: he was humble (vv. 4–7). The Jewish leaders said some wonderful things about this soldier, but he denied them all. "He is worthy!" was their argument, but the centurion said, "I am not worthy!" This was not false modesty on his part; his humility was sincere.

God's work has been damaged more by man's pride than perhaps by any other sin that we commit. "God resists the proud, But gives grace to the humble" (James 4:6; cf. Prov. 3:34). Pride is the sin that transformed the angel Lucifer into the devil, Satan. It was pride that motivated our first forebears to disobey: they wanted to be like God. Pride has brought division to the church and painful disagreement into the family of God. Pride robs God of the glory that belongs only to him.

How easy it would have been for this Roman centurion to be proud! After all, he belonged to the conquering Roman Empire! He was a Roman soldier, an officer, and apparently a man of wealth and influence. Yet he used what he had for others and not for himself. In fact, he did not even feel worthy to go out to meet Jesus personally.

"Under authority." This leads us to a third commendable quality about this man: he was *under* authority. Note the word *also* in verse 8: "For I also am a man placed under authority...." He knew that Jesus was "under authority" and was able to do miracles, for only those who so commissioned should exercise control over others. Just as the centurion could order his soldiers to come and go, so Jesus could command the boy's sickness to depart. The Father gave him that authority!

As leaders in God's work, we exercise authority only because we are under authority. One day we will answer to the Lord for the decisions we have made and the work we have done. Unless we remind ourselves regularly that we are under God's authority, we will be prone to do things our own way for our own glory. But the fact that we are under God's authority should encourage us to trust him and take great steps of faith for his glory.

Faith. Finally, this man was commended by Jesus for his "great faith." In fact, the centurion's faith was so great that even Jesus marveled at it (v. 9). The only other time we find Jesus marveling is at the unbelief of his own people! (Mark 6:6).

You would certainly expect a Jew to have great faith—for, after all, the Jewish nation was especially blessed by God and possessed God's Word. Sad to say, most Jews did not have such faith, and it was a Gentile soldier whose faith Jesus commended. Roman soldiers were trained to be self-sufficient, so this kind of faith was indeed remarkable. The centurion believed in the power of God's Word, that Jesus could "say the word" and the cure would be complete (v. 7).

Are we known for our great faith, or does this Roman soldier put us to shame? Jesus honored his faith and healed the servant boy, and no doubt our Lord was pleased to find such great faith. He certainly had not found it among his own people! Does he find it among us today?

This centurion was not perfect, but he certainly had some wonderful qualities that we would do well to imitate today: concern for others, deep humility, recognition of authority, and great faith. These are the qualities that make for real Christian leadership in the church of Jesus Christ today.

18

Finding the Balance
Luke 10:38–42

I'm just too busy. There isn't enough time!"
These oft-repeated phrases betray the lack of balance and symmetry in our lives. Some of you are probably close to exhaustion! You may feel that your life is like a juggler's plate trick—the plates are spinning, balanced atop the sticks, but you are constantly running to make sure they keep spinning, or else they will crash.

This passage tells how Jesus visited the home of Mary, Martha, and Lazarus to enjoy a good meal and their company. What Jesus found in that home is similar to what happens in our own. The account of Jesus' visit teaches a basic lesson in life: We need to keep our lives in proper balance. There are three dimensions of life to be balanced, and all have to do with our use of time.

1. *Making time for Christ.* Martha wanted dinner to be a culinary delight, and she was working hard to achieve it. Martha wanted each dish ready on time and was feeling pressured. The "quiet dinner" was becoming a source of tension.

Meanwhile, Mary sat quietly, listening to Jesus. His words brought her inner peace and deepened her understanding. What a contrast: Martha, pulled to pieces, with a riot going on inside—and Mary, calm and at ease. The difference? Mary made time for Christ.

Time spent with Jesus is a priceless investment. It is not a luxury; it is a necessity. When we take time to be with Christ each day, what we gain in those moments is lasting; it can never be taken from us (v. 42). The relationship we build with Christ equips us to face the day, calm and unafraid. For those of us whose lives seem dominated by the second hand, is there daily time for the Lord Jesus? There had better be—or we'll be way off balance.

2. *Spending time at work.* God intended that man should work; it is one way to use our abilities and fulfill our potential. Martha gets a lot of criticism, but she was not *all* wrong! People must eat. And there is nothing wrong with preparing and enjoying a good meal. The problem had to do with motives: Martha was trying to impress Jesus, not satisfy his needs.

We must realize that our work responsibilities are not divorced from our service to Christ. Since we are to do our work "heartily, as to the Lord" (Col. 3:23), we cannot divide life into the sacred and the secular. The "secular" becomes "sacred" when done for the Lord. When our work is done for Christ, it becomes an act of worship.

The way we do our work will also reveal whether we have spent time with Christ. Martha was pulled in many directions at once ("distracted") and was internally upset (v. 40). What motivates our work will also show if we have been with Christ, for then we will do it from love, not to impress someone or receive personal gain.

3. *Taking time to enjoy life.* This is the third

dimension needed in a balanced life. Jesus came to this home to relax, not to cause tensions. He wanted to enjoy time with his friends, be among people who loved him. "Only a few things are necessary," he said (v. 42). The simple joys of life provide the deepest satisfactions.

Somehow, Christians seem prone to believe that being worn out is spiritual, that if we are exhausted by serving the Lord, we are good servants. But this is not true! Jesus and the disciples took time to go away for a while and rest (Mark 6:31). Life is not to be "endured," it is to be enjoyed (cf. Eccles. 3:12–13; 9:7–9). If work is not balanced with relaxation, then the life we are living is much less than God intended.

Perhaps it is time to unbend the bow and take time to enjoy the life God has given you. If your work has become a burden, you need to unwind. Here are a few suggestions to help in enjoying life:

Strive for excellence, not perfection. Be satisfied when you have done your best. Remember, only God is perfect.

Live one day at a time (Matt. 6:34).

Build margins into your life. This allows you to handle emergencies without destroying either your agenda or peace of mind.

Learn to laugh at yourself and at life's inconveniences.

Jesus said *we* choose how our lives will be (v. 42). Other people and circumstances do not determine what our lifestyle will be like. Jesus wants our lives to be balanced. And that balance begins with him.

19
Solving Problems God's Way
John 6:1–13

One of the tests of spiritual leadership is how we face and solve problems. Finding a way to feed five thousand people would test the faith and wisdom of any leader! The disciples suggested that Jesus send the people away and let them find their own food, but the Lord rejected that solution. Money was not the answer, although many people in our churches still think that money can solve any problem. Andrew found a lad with a small lunch, but what was that among so many? There are five steps we can take when facing any problem:

We must believe that the Lord has a solution. The key statement in this story is in verse 6: "...for [Jesus] Himself knew what He would do." It is encouraging to us as leaders to know that our Lord already has the solution to every problem. Jesus is never at a loss to know what to do. Our mistake is that we do our best to solve the problems *for* him, when all the while he has a perfect plan and has everything under control.

Of course, it takes faith on our part to admit that the problem even has a solution! When the apostles looked out at that huge crowd and then took stock of their meager resources, they must have been ready to give up. How easy it is for us to look at God through our own limitations, when we ought to be looking at the circumstances from the vantage point of God. When we put God between ourselves and the problem, God gets bigger and the problem gets smaller. But when we put the problem between ourselves and the Lord, it makes the Lord look very small. This, then, is the first step in solving our problems. We must believe that the Lord knows what he is doing and that he has an answer for every problem we face.

We must assess our resources and turn them all over to Christ. What we have may not seem like very much, but it can become more than sufficient if it is put into the hands of the Master. The miracle of feeding the five thousand took place in the hands of Jesus, not in the hands of the disciples. It was Jesus who blessed the bread and fish, Jesus who broke the food, and Jesus who gave it to the men to distribute. Yes, the disciples were a part of the blessing, but the miracle was wholly the Lord's. The second step in solving a problem is to place our assets in Jesus' hands and listen to his guidance.

We must be available to do what Jesus wants us to do. Philip wanted to give the Lord advice about their finances (he was "counting the cost"), but our Lord does not want advice. "For who has known the mind of the LORD? Or who has become His counselor?" (Rom. 11:34). Andrew brought the lad with the lunch, though not quite convinced that it would make any difference! But when Jesus started to give orders, the disciples obeyed—and God made a miracle!

If we trust God while we do the "possible," God

will step in and do the "impossible." Jesus raised Lazarus from the dead, but not until the men had rolled the stone from the door of the tomb. Jesus healed the blind man, but not until the man had gone to the Pool of Siloam and washed the clay from his eyes. Our faith is proved by our obedience. If we are available to Jesus and obedient to his Word, then he can work on our behalf. He does the miracles—we do the serving. God must still use human beings to accomplish his work in this world, and a third step in solving problems involves our availability and willingness to do that work.

We must think first of others. An important step in solving a problem *God's* way is to consider and attend to the needs of others before taking care of our own concerns. No doubt the disciples were also hungry, but it is likely that they served the crowd first and saw to it that nobody went away unsatisfied. After this was accomplished, the men gathered twelve baskets of leftovers that they could use to meet their own needs. This event is a good illustration of Matthew 6:33: "But seek first the kingdom of God and His righteousness, and all these things will be added to you." That is good advice for problem solving!

We must be careful not to waste the blessing. Those baskets of fragments remind us that what we do after the problem is solved is just as important as what we did before the Lord gave us the solution. The final step involves assessment and follow-through. There are lessons to be learned afterward, but apparently the disciples did not learn them (Mark 8:14–21). Perhaps they were so caught up in the miracle—or in eating their own supper—that they failed to take in the spiritual lesson Jesus had placed before them.

There are always dangers of misinterpretation after a great victory. John 6:15 tells us that the excited crowd wanted to take Jesus and make him their king! At that stage in their spiritual lives, the disciples probably would have agreed with the crowd. That was probably why Jesus departed and sent the disciples away. He kept them busy picking up the fragments while he dismissed the adulating crowd.

Christian leadership involves facing and solving problems. This is the way we grow, and this is the way the Lord is glorified. When the problems seem impossible to solve, and when our resources seem inadequate, we must remember that we worship the God of the impossible: "Behold, I am the LORD, the God of all flesh. Is there anything too hard for Me?" (Jer. 32:27). Each of us is either a part of the problem or a part of the answer. Our response ought to be: "Ah, LORD God! Behold, You have made the heavens and the earth by Your great power and outstretched arm. There is nothing too hard for You" (Jer. 32:17).

20
Where the Spirit of the Lord Is...
John 16:7–14

We know that the church was born when the Holy Spirit came at Pentecost (Acts 2). We know that the Holy Spirit dwells in each believer (Rom. 8:9) and that he seeks to produce fruit in each of our lives (Gal. 5:22–23). We know that the Spirit gives gifts to each Christian (1 Cor. 12). What we sometimes are not so sure about is how to tell if the Holy Spirit is truly at work in our church!

Most church programs are good, and they are necessary in the life of a congregation. We praise God for our Sunday school, our choir, our youth programs, and our worship services. But it is healthy to evaluate these activities regularly and ask, "Is the Holy Spirit at work here, or are *we* trying to produce results not necessarily inspired of God?" Activity can become a substitute for real ministry, if we are not careful.

Before our Lord went to the cross, he addressed the disciples on the work the Holy Spirit would do. As we meditate on Jesus' words in John 16, let us look for evidence that the Holy Spirit is truly at work in our fellowship.

If the Spirit is guiding us, we will have a growing

witness. One of the Holy Spirit's ministries today is to convict sinners: "...when He comes, [He] will convict the world concerning sin, and righteousness, and judgment" (v. 8, NASB). As the gospel is preached, as the Scripture is taught, people who do not yet know Jesus as their Savior will be made aware of their sin and the need for salvation.

We have to face some hard questions: How long has it been since someone was saved in our church? Do we take our responsibility to witness seriously? We would not want to get a reputation for condemning people—but we should want to be recognized as a church where people come to know Christ!

This has implications for those of us who have been Christians for some time. If the Spirit is at work, our own lives will be marked by a growing purity. The Holy Spirit produces holiness—and if he is dealing with us about wrong attitudes, or habits, that's a good sign. Maybe he is convicting us to give up something that is "good," in order to give us the best. If the Holy Spirit of God is working, our witness will be growing daily.

If the Spirit is at work in us, we will be guided by the truth. "But when He, the Spirit of truth, comes, He will guide you into all the truth..." (v. 13, NASB). "Truth" here refers to the truth about who Jesus is, and about the work he did and is still doing. Jesus says he *is* the truth (John 14:6), and he also tells us that God's Word is truth (John 17:17). As the Holy Spirit leads us, he will use the Scriptures to instruct and guide us.

It is reassuring to know that we have an objective set of guidelines to follow as we serve Christ. We do not have to guess what God wants us to do. He has told us in the Bible, and the Spirit will direct us to the truths we need for each decision.

If the Holy Spirit is guiding us, we are willing to test our decisions and goals by what Scripture says. For instance, the Bible strongly supports the family. Are we careful to schedule church events and meetings so families are not away from home every night of the week? Sunday is a day of rest, a time for family. Do we enforce that principle? Do the leaders who determine budgets and fiscal policy themselves follow the biblical guidelines about giving? Where the Spirit of the Lord is leading, our activities and decisions will be guided by the truth of Scripture.

When the Spirit is powerfully present among us, we will seek to glorify Christ. The verse that best summarizes the ministry of the Holy Spirit is John 16:14, where Jesus states, "He shall glorify Me...." Everything the Spirit does, every gift he bestows, every insight he reveals, is for the greater glory of the Lord Jesus Christ. The Holy Spirit never draws attention to himself; he directs our attention to Jesus.

When we make decisions, we must always ask, "Will this glorify the Lord?" If we remember to ask that question, it is an evidence of the Spirit's working. After all, only Jesus is worthy of glory, and the only things that will last for eternity are those done for his glory. If we are seeking to build a great name for ourselves, our church, or our business, we will stifle the Spirit in our lives. But if we work to the glory of God, the Spirit will bless!

Is our witness growing? Do we allow ourselves to be guided by God's truth? Is the glory of Christ our highest goal? How we answer these questions will reveal if the ministry of the Holy Spirit is evident here in everything we do.

21
Fishing Without a License
John 21:1–14

Peter and his associates were expert fishermen, yet that night they caught nothing. Do you know why? It was because they were "fishing without a license." Before his death, Jesus had told them to meet him in Galilee (Matt. 26:32; cf. 28:7), but he had not told them to go fishing. In fact, when Jesus first called Peter to be his disciple, Peter and the others had left all to follow the Lord (Luke 5:11). Now it looked as though they were returning to the old life. No wonder they failed.

This is a good lesson for all of us to learn. No matter how experienced or determined we may be, unless the Lord directs us, we will fail. "... without Me," said Jesus, "you can do nothing" (John 15:5). Unless we, as God's workers, get our orders from his Word and seek his blessing in prayer, all of our efforts will be in vain.

Another lesson that we can learn from Peter's mistake is that God's servants must learn how to wait. For some of us, waiting is harder than working! Jesus promised to meet them in Galilee, but he did not arrive when they thought he would. Fishermen never like to sit around and do nothing, so they borrowed a boat and went out on the Sea of Galilee, where they had often gone fishing before.

Satan rejoices when God's servants run ahead of God's will. The enemy encourages impatience. Moses ran ahead of the Lord and killed a man. Joshua ran ahead of the Lord and suffered a humiliating defeat at Ai. King Saul failed to wait for God's timing and as a result lost his crown. "Do not be like the horse or like the mule..." warns Psalm 32:9. The horse wants to rush ahead and the mule wants to lag behind. One is impetuous and the other stubborn, and both can be wrong.

As leaders in God's work, we must learn to wait on the Lord. No matter how exciting an idea might be, it is important that we get God's go-ahead, lest we fish all night and catch nothing. Peter was sincere, but he led his fellow disciples astray, simply because he did not take time to wait for God's direction.

Did you notice that these men failed at doing a familiar thing in familiar waters? They had fished these waters hundreds of times, so what they did that night was nothing new to them. But they failed just the same! Some of us have been church officers for many years. We have attended many meetings and made many decisions. In other words, we are fishing in familiar waters, and we had better be careful lest we become overconfident.

That was the mistake Joshua made when he tried to capture Ai (Josh. 7). He had just won a great victory at Jericho, so the "battle of Ai" did not appear to be too difficult. After all, Joshua had been fighting wars since Israel left Egypt (Exod. 17:8–16), and he was an experienced general. But his familiarity with war made him overconfident, and that led to defeat.

Let us be careful that we do not fail in familiar waters. All of our experience can work against us if we do not wait on the Lord and let him have control.

This story ends on a note of encouragement: Jesus Christ can turn our defeats into victories. In fact, victory may be a lot nearer than we realize. When the disciples cast the nets on the other side of the ship, they caught 153 fish!

How easy it would have been for the Lord to scold his erring disciples. Instead, he blessed them and even fed them. You and I—God's workers—will often make wrong decisions and embark on misguided ventures. Although the Lord may let us go our own way just to teach us a good lesson, he will never leave us or forsake us. He loves us too much for that.

Jesus came to his disciples, even though they failed to recognize him, and he helped them get out of the bad situation they had gotten themselves into by their disobedience. *But first they had to admit that they had failed.* That is important! Once they turned everything over to him, he saw them through. This should not be an excuse for us to disobey, but it is certainly an encouragement whenever we have run ahead of the Lord and desperately need his help.

It is a great privilege to be laborers with and for the Lord. Let us be sure that we get our orders from *him.* It can be very dangerous to go fishing without a license!

22
How to Follow Jesus
John 21:15–23

Peter thought he was a good and loyal follower of Christ. He was the first to confess Jesus as the Messiah (Matt. 16:16). He boasted he would never fall away from Jesus (Mark 14:29–31). Then, on the night of Jesus' betrayal and arrest, Peter became a coward and a traitor. Following Jesus involves much more than making bold theological pronouncements and claims of loyalty.

Since Peter had failed as a "fisher of men," he returned to deep-sea fishing (John 21:3). That went poorly, until Jesus came and provided a great catch of fish. Jesus even cooked breakfast for the disciples. And then it was time for Peter and Jesus to talk. Their conversation was about how to follow Jesus. This is a lesson we all need to learn. To follow Jesus, we must meet the three requirements outlined in this passage:

We need a heart devoted to Christ. Three times, Jesus asked Peter about his love for him (vv. 15–17). Our hearts are the center of our lives. What happens in our hearts—the attitudes there—affects the rest of our lives.

Do we really love Jesus? Before we can follow him, we have to answer that question honestly.

Jesus posed it to Peter three times. In verse 15, Jesus is asking, "Peter, how deeply do you love me?" Peter had boasted that his love was stronger than the other disciples'; now he was learning that we cannot compare ourselves to other believers. We each have our own special relationship with Christ.

In verse 16, Jesus is asking Peter, "Do you love me for who I am?" There was a time when Peter wanted nothing to do with a crucified Christ. He had to learn to love Jesus as he was, not how Peter wanted him to be. Jesus wants us to love the *real* Jesus, not an image of himself.

In verse 17, Jesus is asking, "Do you love me the best you can?" Perhaps our love is not as deep as we might like, but Jesus wants the best we have. He never asks for more than we can give, but he does ask for our best. Our love for Jesus is also tested by our actions. Peter was told: "Feed My sheep."

We need a will submitted to Christ. In the past, Peter had told Jesus what to do (cf. Matt. 16:22). In John 21:18–19, Jesus makes it clear that he alone issues the directives, including the one that Peter was eventually going to give his life in serving Christ (v. 19).

We Christians know the inner struggle over who will govern our lives. We may resent Christ's authority or resist it, but the only way we can follow him is by submitting to him.

Christ told Peter he would die a martyr's death. John's commentary on that statement is that Peter's death would glorify God. That divine glory motivates all Christ's followers. Death makes us afraid, but Christ governs even our death.

The safest place for a Christian to be is in the

will of God. Who plans the agenda for your life? For this church? Do we ask Christ to rubber-stamp decisions we have already made? Or do we ask him to choose the way, guiding us through the Scriptures by his Spirit?

We need eyes that are focused on Christ. Immediately after being told to follow, Peter looked at John and asked, "But Lord, what about this man?" (v. 21). It was normal to ask—but wrong. The only story Christ tells us is our own. He never tells us his will for others. We fill the role of disciple, not of God. Jesus told Peter, in effect: "It's not your concern. Just follow me!" (v. 22).

If you watch Christ, he will watch everyone else. Two of the fastest ways to stop following Christ are to compete with other Christians and compare yourself to them. One of two results follows. Either you get a false sense of pride because you look superior, or you grow discouraged because you seem so poor. But the standard we must measure ourselves by is the Lord Jesus. That is the only accurate way to determine spiritual growth.

If we keep our eyes on Christ, we will not get lost. "Keep your eye on the ball" is an old baseball adage, but every season you see routine plays turned into errors because someone "lost" the ball. Resist the temptation to focus on other Christians rather than on Christ.

Jesus says to us, "Follow me." To do that, our hearts must belong to him, our wills must be yielded to his, and our eyes must see only him. If we are not following Christ, we are behind the wrong leader.

23

When the Holy Spirit Works

Acts 2:1–13

A guest at a summer Bible conference in Canada was so thrilled at the rich lather she enjoyed in her daily bath that she asked the manager if she could purchase a carton of the soap. When she arrived home, she had plenty of soap—but no lather! The secret was not in the soap—it was in the water.

Like this misguided woman, many otherwise sincere people in the church focus on the incidentals instead of the essentials—on the surface instead of the depths. This is especially true when it comes to the doctrine of the Holy Spirit and his coming on the Day of Pentecost. Miraculous things certainly occurred that day, but we must be careful not to see only the outward signs and miss the message in those miracles.

We will better understand what the Spirit of God wants to do for us and for our church if we grasp the meaning of three symbols found in this passage: the wind (v. 2), the fire (v. 3), and the wine (v. 13).

The wind. We are not told where the believers were when the Spirit came. Perhaps they were in the upper room, or they may have been in one of the areas in the temple. Suddenly they heard the sound of a mighty rushing wind. They did not feel the wind; they only heard its sound—but it conveyed to them a sense of life-giving power.

Like the Spirit of God, the wind is invisible but powerful. In both Hebrew and Greek, the word for "wind" is the same as the word for "Spirit." Jesus compared the working of the Spirit to the mysterious moving of the wind (John 3:8). You can feel the wind and see what it does, but you cannot explain it or control it.

The wind is a source of life. Without the moving of the wind in our world, living things would die. The wind brings in freshness and helps to carry away pollution. How we need the "wind of the Spirit" in our churches today! It is so easy for us to collect stale air and even get used to it. We need the power and freshness of the wind of heaven to blow upon us.

The fire. The Holy Spirit is also symbolized by the fire. Note that the people saw "tongues of fire." G. Campbell Morgan said that the tongue of fire is the best image of the church because it expresses what the ministry of the church really is: to tell the message of the gospel to the whole world.

When you think of fire, you think of purity. When the Spirit of God is working, he will expose sin and seek to burn it away. In fact, one of the names of the Holy Spirit is "spirit of burning" (Isa. 4:4). But fire also reminds you of warmth, and when the Spirit controls us, we will have a greater love for each other and for the Lord.

Fire speaks of power, and we need the Spirit's

power if we are to witness for Christ (Acts 1:8). Fire also gives illumination. The Spirit of God gives light to God's Word and also to our path as we seek to follow God's leading.

When you combine fire and wind, you have a blaze! "I came to send fire upon the earth...!" said the Lord Jesus (Luke 12:49). God wants us to share this fire with the whole world.

The wine. The third picture of the Spirit is wine. Some of the skeptical people in the crowd said of the believers, "They are full of new wine" (v. 13). Why did they say that? Because they heard the Spirit-filled Christians praising God for his wonderful works and doing so in all the languages spoken by "devout men from every nation under heaven." It was indeed a miracle!

If a group of unsaved people visited a worship service in the average church of today, it is doubtful that they would accuse the worshipers of being drunk! Embalmed, perhaps, but not drunk! Why? Because we are not filled with the Spirit and overflowing with praise to God. Paul commands us to be filled with the Spirit (Eph. 5:18), and he points out that one of the evidences of this fullness is the singing of praises to the Lord. To those Jews, wine was a symbol of joy (*see* Ps. 104:15)—and one fruit of the Spirit is joy (Gal. 5:22).

Here, then, are three wonderful gifts the Spirit wants to bring to our lives and to our church: the freshness and power of the wind, the purity and warmth of the fire, and the joy that comes with his fullness. To be sure, all things must be done "decently and in order" (1 Cor. 14:40), and we must beware of manufactured substitutes. But if we will open our lives to the Spirit and let him have control, he will bring a new freshness and power and joy to our lives, and Jesus Christ will be glorified.

24
Cultivating
the Right Attitude
Romans 12:16

Having a good attitude makes life better. If you enjoy your work, it is easy to begin the day with a positive outlook. But if you hate cleaning house and wake to a domestic disaster area—or dislike your boss and your job's routine—you may go through the day with a frown and a thunder-cloud over your head!

When people live and work together, it is inevitable that there will be some conflict. People are individuals and often disagree, whether it's about music, TV, the dinner menu, or a Scripture version. Disagreements among believers can produce bad attitudes toward the church or other Christians. Yet we are told that the people of God are to be marked by their unity. Cultivating the right attitudes can help preserve unity and fellowship, even when we don't agree about specifics.

Romans 12:16 reads "Be of the same mind toward one another; do not be haughty in mind, but associate with the lowly. Do not be wise in your own estimation" (NASB). In this verse, Paul indicates three attitudes that each Christian should cultivate.

Harmony. We need, first of all, to cultivate an attitude of harmony. When Paul tells us to "be of the same mind," he is instructing us to emphasize what we have in common. We have the same Father in heaven and the same Savior, and the same Holy Spirit indwells us. We are bound together by submitting ourselves to the authority of Scripture. As members of our church, we share a common ministry and mutual goals.

Harmony is a fragile quality. It takes only one violin out of tune to make the entire string section of an orchestra sound discordant. One Christian with a sour attitude can disrupt a church. Jealousy can wreck the spirit of unity. Tolerating sin will disrupt harmony among believers, as will a lack of prayer or love. Since we need harmony, we must recognize that it is possible to disagree without being disagreeable (ways to achieve that are explained in our next chapter).

Humility. Next, Paul tells us not to be "haughty in mind." We need to cultivate an attitude of humility. This is a gentle reminder that no matter what we have achieved or experienced, no believer is superior to any other believer. This is where we need to follow closely the example of our Lord Jesus (Phil. 2:5–8). Jesus submitted to the Father's will; he became a servant and was obedient unto death. *That* is humility, and that is the attitude we must develop.

Pride is a destroyer. When one singer in a choir begins to think his or her ability is superior to everyone else's, trouble is brewing. When individual pastors or deacons feel that what they are doing is the most important thing in the church, look out. The church of Jesus Christ is not to be a classed society or have a caste system. When the Spirit came and the church was born, all distinctions were swept away: "There is neither Jew nor Greek, there is neither slave nor free man, there is neither male nor female; for you are all one in Christ Jesus" (Gal. 3:28, NASB).

God has gifted each Christian; each person and his or her gifts are necessary. It takes all God's people to make up the body of Christ, and everyone is as important as any other.

Honesty. A third attitude we must cultivate is honesty—"Do not be wise in your own estimation." The New International Version puts it "Do not be conceited." No one likes a know-it-all, but no one really likes a doormat, either.

God has given some people beautiful voices to use in glorifying God. When a gifted person sings and it blesses us, we should thank the singer. But some in the audience might omit the thanks, implying that the performance was not so great. That's not being honest! God gave the gift, so we should be open in our appreciation. Another singer might say, "Thank you" in a grudging tone, indicating that thanks are not really warranted. That is not being honest, either. God's gifts must not be disparaged in another. We must honestly recognize the gifts God has given to all, thank him for them, and use them to his glory.

Having an attitude of honesty means you will be willing to submit your ideas and plans to other Christians for evaluation. There is wisdom among many counselors, says the proverb. Many Christians have avoided embarrassment or failure because they were willing to listen to an honest critique.

These three attitudes—harmony, humility, and

93

honesty—really reflect the most important attitude of all, our attitude toward the Lord Jesus. Where people love the Lord and give him the highest place, there you will find harmony, humility, and honesty in full measure.

25

When Good People Disagree

Romans 14

Bible accounts, church history, and our own personal experiences, all bear witness to the fact that good and godly people have their disagreements. However, variances of opinion over minor matters must not be allowed to develop into divisions that create major problems and schisms in the body of Christ. We must learn to disagree without being disagreeable if we are to serve the Lord together and glorify his name.

The believers in the Roman assemblies to whom Paul wrote were not in agreement over such matters as when to worship and what to eat. Many Jewish believers still held to some of their traditional diets and holy days, while the Gentiles in the assemblies enjoyed their greater liberty in Christ. How did Paul counsel them? Certainly not by giving them a list of rules! Laws can manufacture uniformity, but they can never produce unity. No, Paul appealed to their love and gave them some abiding principles to guide them in their personal relationships. From the principles in Romans 14 we can draw up a list of "inventory questions" to help us examine and strengthen our own relationships when we find ourselves disagreeing.

95

1. *What is my heart's attitude toward my brother?* (vv. 1–4). If we start with pride, it will lead to judging, and that will only create more disagreements and divisions. We must start with love and mutual esteem. The stronger believers must not despise the weaker ones, and neither must the weaker judge the stronger. So long as there is an attitude of love and mutual acceptance, we can pray together, talk over our differences, and come to a satisfactory conclusion—for "love is the fulfillment of the law" (v. 10).

2. *Do I really know the facts?* (v. 5). Too often we make our decisions on the basis of prejudice and personal opinion rather than on the basis of fact and biblical revelation. If your mind is already made up, then there is no sense even listening to your brother when he presents his side of the issue! The honest believer cannot be "fully convinced" until he has fully examined the matter from all sides.

3. *Am I seeking to please God or myself?* (vv. 6–9). The key idea in these verses is that we are the Lord's, and therefore we must live to please him. The church does not belong to us; it belongs to the Lord. We must remember this whenever we call it "our" church. All believers belong to the Lord, and we must be careful how we treat God's precious property. It is so easy for us to fool ourselves into thinking that our will is really God's will! If we sincerely desire to please the Lord, then we will not be afraid to listen to others and get another view of the matter.

4. *Am I ready to give account to God?* (vv. 10–12). It is one thing to discuss a matter with a committee

or another believer, but what will I say when I face Jesus Christ? What a solemn hour that will be! I need to remind myself that I will not give an account for *you*, but only for myself. At that accounting, nothing will be hidden, including the motives of our hearts. You and I today need to behave ourselves in such a way that we will not be ashamed when this matter comes up as we "stand before the judgment seat of Christ."

5. *Am I injuring others by my attitudes or words?* (vv. 13–15). What good is it to be right in my thinking if I am wrong in my words or attitudes? Can I build up the church by tearing down a fellow believer? This is not to suggest that we modify Bible truth just to please other people, but it does urge us to "speak the truth in love" (Eph. 4:15), so that nobody is caused to stumble. To grieve my brother, or to cause him to stumble, is to act unlike Jesus Christ, who died for that brother.

6. *Do I have the right priorities?* (vv. 16–21). The kingdom of God is not built on minor matters such as food and drink. What is really important is the spiritual quality of our lives and our ministry— righteousness, peace, joy, the ministry of the Spirit of God. The essential ingredient is not that we agree on everything, but that we promote the peace of God's people as we build up one another in the Lord. This does not mean "peace at any price," because God's wisdom is "first pure, then peaceable" (James 3:17). What it does mean is that we must not destroy God's work over some minor matter. We must avoid becoming like the Pharisees,

97

who strained out a little gnat but failed to see the camel—and swallowed it (Matt. 23:24)!

7. *Am I really living by faith?* (vv. 22–23). Do I have any doubts at all that perhaps I may be wrong? To live by faith means to have the Word of God tell us what to do, and to have the witness of the Spirit of God within. Not all believers are at the same level of either faith or knowledge, and we must make allowances. If God has brought me to a higher level than my brother's, then I must use my position to pull him up—not to knock him down! I cannot force him to grow in his faith, but I can encourage him by loving him and not trying to impose my faith on him by requiring compliance to a set of rules.

Yes, Christians do have differences; but those differences ought to be opportunities for building and not for battling. Let us not examine one another; rather, let us examine our own hearts and lives to make sure *we* are right with the Lord. Then we will be able to pray together, talk together, and make the right decisions to the glory of God.

26

An Honest Assessment
1 Corinthians 3:9–17

We may not think much about "expectations," but they influence us every day. If you were expecting a beautiful, sunny day and there was rain, you get grumpy. If the boss called you into a meeting and you were expecting criticism but then received a raise, you are on top of the world.

Each of us has expectations of the church and its leaders. Our expectations determine, to a large degree, whether or not we are happy in church. In 1 Corinthians 3:9–23, Paul reminds us that the church is a building—and it is God's, not ours. The expectations that matter most for a church are God's!

This passage reveals God's blueprint for a church and helps us understand what he expects to see in our church. We need to assess ourselves and see how we measure up. The simplest way would be to ask three questions:

1. *What are we building on?* In verses 10–11, Paul discusses the foundation of the building. The only foundation to build on is Jesus Christ (v. 11). The foundation is the most important part of any structure. If the foundation is wrong, nothing else will be right. The building will be stable only if

the foundation is right. If the foundation crumbles, so does everything else.

Are we building on the truth that Jesus Christ is God's Son, who died on Calvary for our sins and rose again to give us eternal life? Do we test our programs, our budget, our worship, our music, by the standards of God's Word? A foundation must go deep to support a large building. Our foundation must be deeply imbedded in the person of Jesus. Our church cannot go any deeper than we go spiritually as individuals.

2. *What are we building with?* Paul goes on to discuss in verses 12–15 the kind of materials that are used in the process of construction. Paul first gives us two categories of materials: those you have to dig for (gold, silver, precious stones), and those that are ready at hand (wood, hay, straw). God looks for quality, value, and durability—and building that into a church takes time.

When you build a corporation in the secular world, you do it with money, power, position, reputation, and manipulation. God builds his church in opposite fashion: by prayer, giving, sacrifice, the Scriptures, the ministry of the Holy Spirit, kindness, and service. These "invisible" materials, built into the church through our lives, contribute to the endurance of the eternal church.

A day of testing is going to come (v. 13), and the quality of our material will be demonstrated. If we have merely done what was convenient or expedient, there may not be much left. If we have put Christ first, obeyed the Scriptures, prayed, and sacrificed, there will be a reward (v. 14).

3. *What are we building for?* Paul then pictures

100

the church as the temple of God, where the Spirit of God lives, and confronts us with this third question. The church is the place where God dwells, where he is to be worshiped. He is to be the One who receives glory. The church's reason for existing is to glorify the King of kings and Lord of lords.

It is possible for men and women to use a church for their own ends. They want to build a reputation as a great church or gain recognition as "spiritual" leaders. Here's a good test to discover what we are building for: When something good happens, who gets the credit?

Paul gives a warning in verse 17: "If any man defiles the temple of God, God will destroy him." The church is to be treated with respect; she is *Christ's* building, *Christ's* bride. If we are not motivated to glorify God, we may be doing more demolition than construction.

In building the church, Jesus Christ is the foundation; spiritual truth and integrity are the materials; God's glory is the goal. Now we know God's expectations. How does *our* church measure up?

27

To the Glory of God

1 Corinthians 10:31

Therefore, whether you eat or drink, or whatever you do, do all to the glory of God." As we prepare to conduct the business of the church, we ought to consider this command carefully. Each decision we make, every dollar we spend, should bring glory to our heavenly Father.

Surely we know why everything must glorify God! He is the greatest Person in the universe; he deserves our best and highest. He is the only Being *worthy* of glory. God created us to glorify him, and we are at our best as human beings only when we glorify God. Giving him glory is the only proper response to salvation. Finally, only what is done to the glory of God will last. Everything done for the glory of man eventually fades and falls, but God's glory is eternal.

The command to glorify God in all we do forces us to examine our ministry closely. We can apply this command by asking three questions about our activities in the church:

1. *Why are we doing this?* Seeking God's glory in all we do forces us to examine our motives. If we are going to serve God, we have to do it from the right motivation.

Motives can be a cloudy area. Many times we are unsure of the reasons we do or say what we do. Even when we think our motives are pure, they may be self-serving. Near the end of his reign, King David took a census of his people. His motive was pride—he wanted to glorify David, not God. After the people had been numbered, David realized his sin. God sent a plague, and seventy thousand men died (2 Sam. 24).

Ananias and Sapphira sold some land and gave a gift to the church (Acts 5:1–11). They pretended to give the entire proceeds to the church, when in fact they kept some for themselves. The motivation for this lie was greed and a desire to be considered as generous as Barnabas (Acts 4:36–37). God was not glorified, and it cost Ananias and Sapphira their lives.

When we consider the budget, we must weigh our motives for spending or cutting. Perhaps a missionary needs and deserves more support, but someone with a personal grudge opposes the expenditure. In the area of music, those who sing and play should direct attention to Jesus Christ, not themselves. As best we know how, we must be sure we are motivated by love for Christ.

2. *How godly are our methods?* Our methods also come under scrutiny when we desire to glorify God. We must not do a "good thing for God" in a bad way. When Israel needed water, God instructed Moses to speak to a rock, and water would be provided (Num. 20:8). Moses grew angry with the people and hit the rock instead of speaking to it (vv. 9–11). God still gave water, but because Moses did

103

not honor God before the people, he was denied entrance to the Promised Land.

God's work must be done God's way. Churches should follow sound business practices, but they must not be run like a business in the secular world. There is a world of difference between business and ministry. Souls should be won through love and prayerful witnessing, not through high-pressure salesmanship. The methods we employ for raising and handling finances, for recruiting staff, for handling discipline matters, must all conform to Scripture.

Sometimes God's methods surprise—and worry—us. Gideon was told to fight the enemy with only three hundred men, pitchers and torchers, and trumpets. An unlikely arsenal—but it worked! (Judg. 7).

3. *What are we trying to achieve?* As we seek to glorify God, we must also examine our goals. For some ministries, their primary goal is to project a successful image and keep the income rolling in. Others appear to exist to promote one person, a human leader. Yet the command we are considering tells us our goal is to lift up *God*.

When we lose sight of that goal, we are bound to end up in trouble. Remember the incident in Exodus 32 where Aaron made the golden calf? What was his goal? Not to keep the people faithful to Jehovah. Not to obey God's law. He did it to escape a tense situation. Moses had been gone a long time on Mount Sinai, and the people were pressuring Aaron to do something. What he did damaged his own testimony, as well as failing to glorify God. When the goal is to glorify God, we will do what is right, not what is easy.

104

John wrote about a church leader named Diotrephes (3 John 9–10). It seems that Diotrephes was not concerned with God's glory, he was only occupied by the pursuit of personal power. His words and actions caused problems in the church. Where God is glorified, there is harmony.

We can have lesser goals than God's glory—and we can reach them. But what is achieved will not last. Only what is done for Christ will endure (1 Cor. 3:14–15). We need a sense of the eternal as we establish goals—and what is done for God *is* eternal.

As we plan worship services, establish budgets, teach classes, share our faith, sing in the choir, solve problems—our motives, methods, and goals must bring glory to God.

28

Weary in "Well Doing"?
1 Corinthians 15:58; 2 Thessalonians 3:13

People never get tired of doing good things, do they? Think about tending your garden. It's fun in the early spring, when the first green shoots are up. But what about in August, when the weeds and bugs are thick? Or doing dishes—an important job but rather dull after the first decade. And mowing your lawn is good and necessary, but you can't wait for your son to be old enough to do it!

It is a fact of life that we do get tired of doing things that are worthwhile. Playing the organ is vital to worship, but fingers grow weary. Sunday school is a significant ministry, but teachers need vacations. Nursery help is a necessity, but even the most dedicated nursery worker longs for escape. When those times of tiredness come, how should we handle it? Let us try to answer two questions:

Why do we grow weary? There are several reasons for weariness. Sometimes we are just physically tired. Elijah thought God had abandoned him and the world was against him, and he wanted to die (1 Kings 19:4). His problem was physical exhaustion, since he had had quite a few busy days (cf. 1 Kings 18). God provided Elijah with rest and refreshment, and he was able to go on.

106

Weariness can also have emotional causes. Perhaps you have worked hard with your Sunday-school class, but have seen no lasting results. Discouragement sets in, and if there is no improvement, we begin to despair. Some of the Thessalonian believers were growing weary because other Christians were not doing their share (2 Thess. 3:10–13). When it seems as if you are the only person who cares, it is easy to grow weary of well doing.

It may be that you have gone through a recent crisis. A loved one has died, or you had to relocate, or some pleasant experience you anticipated did not happen. These experiences take an emotional toll, and if we try to carry on as usual with an extra burden, weariness can develop in a hurry.

Finally, there are spiritual causes for weariness in well doing. In Malachi 1:13, God accuses his people of merely going through the motions of worship. They followed the routine, but were neither spiritually nor emotionally involved with God. When we lose touch with God, we lose the sense of doing a vital work for him. Examine the state of your quiet time to see if something other than the Lord Jesus occupies the throne of your life.

How can we overcome weariness? When you identify signs of being "weary in well doing," don't panic. And don't feel guilty! It happens to all of us. Recognize that times of weariness will come, but they don't have to stay. Get some extra sleep, spend some time praying, take off a session from teaching and become a student again. Meditate on the following spiritual encouragements, and let them sink deep into your heart:

1. Remember that what you do is for God. Since

we are doing "the work of the Lord" (1 Cor. 15:58), he is responsible for the results. God knows the part you play. He sees how faithfully you serve. Nothing you do is overlooked. Even if no one else notices your service, your heavenly Father sees and cares.

2. Remember that what you do is helpful. In the same verse of 1 Corinthians, Paul assures you that "your labor is not in vain in the Lord." As long as you are motivated by love for Christ and his glory, God will bless what you do. We always do more good than we realize. It is the nature of spiritual work that results are seen only with the passing of time. Don't give up on your Bible class—work and wait! In five years, the teen who is breaking your heart may have been called as a missionary.

3. Remember that what you do for God always bears fruit: "...in due season we shall reap, if we do not lose heart" (Gal. 6:9). It takes time to reach the harvest. If we have faithfully planted the seed, the harvest *will* come. And one of the laws of the harvest is that we reap more than we planted. Prayers and kindnesses, faithfulness to Christ, and reliance on the Spirit will produce beautiful fruit.

These Scriptures are not asking us to do more; they are encouraging us to continue to do well what we have been doing. There will be times when we wonder if it is all worth the effort, if quitting is not wiser. Remember: we do it for God, and in his strength there will be a rich harvest.

29

Act Your Age!
1 Corinthians 16:13–14

Here, Paul's exhortation to "quit you like men" (KJV) simply means, in everyday language, "Act your age! Be an adult! Don't act like a baby!" It was Paul's final reminder to the Corinthians that it was time for them to grow up. They had been hearing the message of salvation long enough and been given many wonderful opportunities for maturing in the Lord, and yet they were still spiritual infants (1 Cor. 3:1–4). No wonder they had so many problems in their fellowship!

God's all-important work demands the best that we can give it. The church is not ministering on a playground for infants; it is standing on a battle-ground where we must confront the attacks of the enemy and seek to be "more than conquerors" to God's glory (Rom. 8:37). We know the price that Jesus paid that we might be a part of his church, and we dare not take this for granted. Service is serious business.

As never before, God's church needs adult-minded leadership. In these brief verses, Paul points the way to spiritual maturity in the Lord's service, by giving us four personal admonitions.

Keep your eyes open. "Watch" means "Be alert!

109

Be on guard!" Jesus had called the Pharisees "blind leaders of the blind" (Matt. 15:14), and the people must have laughed at the irony of his words. While we are amazed at what blind people can accomplish, we would prefer to have guides who can see where they are going and detect whatever dangers may lie ahead.

Satan is a lion, always on the prowl (1 Peter 5:8). Blowing around us are constant "winds of doctrine" that can bring problems to the church (Eph. 4:14). Just a small amount of "old leaven" can get into a church and infect the fellowship's "bread of sincerity and truth" (1 Cor. 5:6–8). As leaders, we must keep our eyes open and be wary of the dangers around us.

But we must also be alert to opportunities for ministry. "...lift up your eyes and look at the fields, for they are already white for harvest!" (John 4:35). All around us are open doors, and we must enter them before they are closed. Too often we who lead God's work are so content with "business as usual" that we fail to see the exciting new opportunities God has set before us.

Plant your feet firmly and stand! Paul tells us to "stand fast in the faith." How and where we stand determines how we walk and where we work. Some Christians want to please everybody, so they never take a definite stand on anything. But, as leaders, we must take a position so that those who follow will know where we stand and thus where we lead. Martin Luther's "Here I stand, I can do none other, so help me God!" is a good example for us to follow.

It would do us good to examine our doctrinal

position and to reaffirm its validity. Reviewing the principles by which we operate will determine whether we are obeying the Word of God. To be sure, there are areas in every ministry where good and godly people may disagree, but there are also basic truths on which all of us must agree and stand firmly together. Only if we know where we stand, and if we stand as one, can we defeat the enemy and conquer new territory for Christ and the gospel.

Have a courageous heart! Paul's third admonition in verse 13 is "be brave, be strong." It takes courage to serve God. An old proverb notes that "nothing is impossible to a willing heart." The early Christians knew that their witness for Christ would bring official opposition, persecution, and perhaps even martyrdom, but they courageously served the Lord just the same. Courage dismisses the obstacles, seeing only the goal. If we lack courage, whatever virtues and abilities we have are relatively useless. It takes courage and faith to dedicate our gifts toward accomplishing what God has for us to do.

A coward has been defined by Ambrose Bierce as "one who in a perilous emergency thinks with his legs." Paul tells us to stand firmly on our feet! And the only way to take that stance is by listening to a heart that is filled with courage from the Lord.

Cultivate a loving attitude. "Let all that you do be done with love" (v. 14). Unless courage and love live in the same heart, both will suffer. Courage prevents love from degenerating into shallow sentiment, and love enables courage to be constructive and not destructive. We see both of these qualities so beautifully displayed in the life of our Lord Jesus

111

Christ. He was compassionately courageous in all that he did.

One of the major emphases in 1 Corinthians is our love for one another, and 1 Corinthians 13 is perhaps the greatest passage ever written about love. The believers in Corinth had many gifts of the Spirit, but they lacked the graces of the Spirit. They were not using their gifts as tools to build with, but as toys to play with—and even as weapons to fight with! The result was division in the church, and with that division came defilement and disgrace.

True leadership demands love. Otherwise that leadership becomes selfish and demanding. The true shepherd goes before the flock and *leads* the sheep, not behind the flock to drive or beat it along. Even when we make hard decisions or disagree, we must do so in love. Someone has well said that "love is the circulatory system of the spiritual body." Cut off the circulation and the body becomes sick, and it could die.

These two verses are a call for Christian maturity in leadership. Sir Winston Churchill once defined responsibility as "the price of greatness." God has called us to carry responsibilities in his church, and this involves maturity. Effective leaders are not interested in personal greatness but only in bringing glory to the Lord Jesus Christ. Let us be sure that we have "put away childish things" (1 Cor. 13:11) and are growing more like the Lord Jesus Christ. We will therefore be better prepared to do his work.

30

When God Changes Our Plans

2 Corinthians 1:12–20

Some of the people in the Corinthian church were upset with Paul because he had twice changed his travel plans and disappointed them. He had originally promised to spend the winter in Corinth and then travel to Judea to deliver the special "relief offering" from the Gentile churches (1 Cor. 16:5–6). But then he had revised his plans and promised the church he would make *two* stops at Corinth before going to Jerusalem (2 Cor. 1:15–16). After building up their hopes, Paul finally ended up making a quick, painful visit to Corinth in an attempt to solve the problems in the church. All their expectations were unfulfilled, and critical factions in the church took these changes as evidences that Paul was indecisive and unstable. They were convinced that Paul could not be trusted. In this passage, Paul seeks understanding as he allays their doubts about his sincerity.

God's servants must occasionally change their plans as they do God's work, and this can result in their being misunderstood. Of course, in every group there are those who are only looking for something to criticize, and the Corinthian church was no exception. Some accused Paul of being insincere and careless with the truth. Apparently they said that his letters had a double meaning, that his "yes" meant "no," and his "no" meant "yes" (v. 17). Paul learned that leadership is never easy and is especially difficult when you have to change your plans.

This critical situation in Paul's ministry reminds us that we who are God's servants must know how to handle the misunderstanding and criticism that may follow when there are unavoidable changes in our plans. When we face that kind of situation, it is good for us to stop and take inventory to make certain we are really in God's will. From Paul's inspired words, let us ask four important questions:

1. *Is our conscience clear?* (vv. 12–13). The word *conscience* means "to know with." The conscience is the inner "spiritual judge" that approves when we do what is right and disapproves when we do what is wrong. The conscience is the window that lets in the light of God's truth. If the window is clean, the light shines through brightly, and we know what is right and what is wrong. If the window is dirty, the light is partially deflected, and conscience can lead us astray. The Bible calls this a "defiled" conscience (1 Cor. 8:7; Titus 1:15).

No matter what his critics said, Paul was sure that his conscience was clear. Some of the people at Corinth misunderstood what Paul had said and done, but God knew that his servant was acting in "godly sincerity." Paul had not been practicing duplicity; he stood ready to defend his integrity.

It is important that we as leaders follow Paul's example and "always strive to have a conscience without offense toward God and men." No Chris-

114

tian can maintain a clear conscience while guilty of scheming and lying. Billy Graham has said that many people "follow their conscience the way they follow a wheelbarrow: they push it in whatever direction they want it to go!"

"Conscience and reputation are two things," said Saint Augustine. "Conscience is due to yourself, reputation to your neighbor." There may be times when our reputation will suffer because we are true to our conscience! We may lose our reputation, but we will keep our character, and that is what really counts.

2. *Can we honestly face the Lord?* *(v. 14)*. In this verse, "the day of the Lord" refers to that time when Christ will return and we will stand before him for our works to be judged. We may be able to fool others and even ourselves, but we will never be able to fool the Lord.

It is so important that we work today in the light of the Lord's return, that we live with eternity's values in view. It is encouraging to us to know that God knows the truth about our lives and ministries, and that he will balance the books at the judgment seat of Christ. People may misunderstand us, but God is always watching our hearts and our motives. He knows the truth.

3. *Are we serious about God's will?* (vv. 17–18). From the very beginning of his planning, Paul wanted only the will of God. "I hope to stay a while with you, if the Lord permits" is what he had written to them (1 Cor. 16:7), and he meant this sincerely. Paul was too good a Christian to take God's will lightly or treat it with worldly disdain. To him, the will of God was uppermost in all his plans.

115

But even this inspired apostle had to confess that he did not always know how to pray about God's will (Rom. 8:26). He sought God's guidance, but sometimes his movements were thwarted by the Spirit of God (Acts 16:6–8). Paul moved a step at a time and lived each day as it came, honestly seeking the direction of the Lord.

God sees our hearts. He knows the seriousness of our dedication and our purpose. We can but make the best decisions we can, with the information and illumination that we have. We must leave the rest with the Lord. If we are serious, God will guide us.

4. *Are we trusting God's Word?* (vv. 19–20). His accusers claimed that Paul's word could not be trusted—that when he said, "Yes, I will come," he really meant the opposite. Of course, this was a serious charge to bring against a gospel preacher, because a dedicated man of God must not separate his words from his life and character. Our "walk" and our "talk" must agree, lest we be considered hypocrites.

Paul made it clear that all of God's promises are fulfilled in Christ. He is God's great "Yes!" When we trust his Word, we say a believing "Amen!" to what God has revealed in his Son. If we are trusting God's Word as we make our decisions, and depending on his faithfulness, we can go ahead with confidence, even though the situation changes and plans must be rearranged.

Faithful leadership is not easy. Leaders who want to glorify God and do his will are often criticized and misunderstood. Even the most devoted leaders can and do make mistakes. Let us examine our hearts honestly and make certain that we are right with God. If we are, then he will take care of the rest.

116

31

Growing in Gratitude

2 Corinthians 9:15

God's people ought to be people who are grateful. Many Christians, it seems, take their blessings for granted, instead of responding with gratitude. A spirit of thankfulness should mark our lives. "Thanks be to God for His indescribable gift!" Paul wrote in this verse. In meditating on this prayer of thanksgiving, we can discover several ways to increase our level of gratitude:

Never get used to your blessings. Since Paul never stopped being amazed that the Father gave his Son, the wonder the apostle felt produced a spirit of continual thanksgiving. Complaining is easy—we gripe about many things each day. It takes little effort or special talent to be a grumbler. But it does take spiritual character to give thanks!

At the first Thanksgiving celebrated by the Pilgrims, there seemed more to complain about than to give thanks for. Many of the people had died, the harvest was disappointing, and their community house had burned. But they still set aside a day to celebrate God's provision and goodness. Their spiritual insight let them discover blessings in the midst of their trials.

Consider all that we enjoy each day—and how

117

often we enjoy this bounty without appreciation. Let us count every blessing and be joyful.

Remember that all blessings come from God. "Thanks be to God," says Paul. All we have comes as a gift from God. We received everything we possess through his grace. When we have learned to live under grace, we acknowledge God's provision for us. Praying together over a meal is one simple way to cultivate the habit of giving thanks to God.

We tend to think of blessings as pleasurable—unexpected income, avoiding some difficult situation, having our prayers answered according to our expectations. But even life's trials bring forth our gratitude if we accept them as from the heavenly Father, sent for our good. The phrase "sacrifice of thanksgiving" takes on a deeper meaning when we have been able to offer thanks to God from the valley, where he was faithful.

Remember that the best blessings are spiritual. We usually give thanks for the blessings we can see and touch, but the spiritual realities are far richer. The "indescribable gift" Paul speaks of is the Lord Jesus, the Source of all the blessings we receive. Consider a few. Because of Jesus, we can call God our Father; we have the assurance of sins forgiven and the presence of the Holy Spirit in us. Jesus brings the hope of heaven, the privilege of prayer, the experience of God's love. These are the blessings that make one truly wealthy. Avoid the mistake of measuring your fortune in terms of dollars and cents. The best blessings are spiritual!

Remember to share your blessings. Paul's thanksgiving concludes a passage where he has reminded the Corinthians of their blessings, which God had

118

provided and Paul had shared. In response, the Corinthians were taking an offering to give to the saints in Jerusalem. It is a basic principle with God's people that blessings are to be shared, not hoarded (vv. 6–7).

We best express our gratitude when we give to someone else, when we maintain the emphasis on the "giving" part of "thanksgiving." How do we share our blessings? Not only in material ways, but with our words as we praise God and encourage others. "Thank you" should be a staple in our vocabulary. Everyday kindnesses also reveal our spirit of thanksgiving. "It is more blessed to give than to receive," said Jesus. Giving our time or ability, serving where there are needs, offering hope and encouragement—these are the evidences of a grateful heart.

Be careful not to limit the giving of thanks to the fourth Thursday of November. It is a quality that must mark our lives *always*. Giving thanks and praise is something we must learn—a skill we acquire as the Holy Spirit focuses our attention on the Lord Jesus. And while we are concentrating on Christ, we will be growing in gratitude each day.

32

"It's Always Too Soon to Quit!"

Galatians 6:9

The late president of Wheaton (Illinois) College, Dr. V. Raymond Edman, often reminded the students that "it's always too soon to quit!" This is excellent advice, not only for students, but for anybody who is seeking to serve the Lord and accomplish his work. In the Lord's service, it is *never* time to slacken our efforts!

Paul had this same idea in mind when he wrote, "And let us not grow weary while doing good, for in due season we shall reap if we do not lose heart" (Gal. 6:9). Whenever we are tempted to do less than our best, or perhaps to quit completely, we ought to remember this verse and the truths that it contains. Here Paul talks about a privilege, a peril, and a promise.

Paul speaks about *a privilege*—"doing good." That is what Christian life and service are all about. "Let your light so shine before men, that they may see your good works and glorify your Father in heaven" (Matt. 5:16). We Christians are not only believers; we are behavers. We do the will of God and the work of God for the glory of God.

Jesus himself "went about doing good" (Acts 10:38). When you and I are involved in good works, we are following in the steps of the Master. "But be doers of the word, and not hearers only..." James admonished (1:22). "For it is God who works in you both to will and to do for His good pleasure" (Phil. 2:13). Although we are certainly not saved by doing good works, we do prove the reality of our salvation by investing our lives in good works.

Sometimes believers, especially leaders in the church, are prone to look at service as a burden or a chore. Christian ministry is not easy; it demands time and toil and energy. We must realize, however, that ministry is a privilege! Otherwise, we will start to get bitter and critical, and then our work will lose God's blessing. No matter how much sacrifice God calls us to make, we must keep in mind that serving Jesus Christ in any capacity is a wonderful privilege.

Paul also speaks about *a peril*—the danger of growing "weary" in serving the Lord. It has often been said that though we get weary *in* the Lord's work, we must never get weary *of* the Lord's work. When that happens, we cease to be God's joyful servants. We then become drudges who are miserable in what we do and help to make others just as miserable. We mimic the priests whom Malachi warned—men who did not give God their best and said of their service, "Oh, what a weariness!" (Mal. 1:13).

The kind of weariness Paul is talking about has nothing to do with a tired body. It is a weariness of the mind and heart, a loss of excitement and challenge, which produces a ministry that is dull, lifeless, routine, and ineffective. We stop planning ahead and are merely content to monitor "business as

121

usual." We have no joy in service, and we stop making sacrifices. Before long, we start to get critical and resentful. Like the elder brother in our Lord's parable (Luke 15:25–32), we can be busy in the field and even faithful to the Father, but still be a drudge who finds no joy in ministry.

If you keep reminding yourself that it is a privilege to serve the Lord, you are not likely to grow weary in well doing. Say to yourself, "To think that God has chosen me to be his servant!" and you will not lose the wonder of it all.

Finally, Paul speaks about *a promise*—"for in due season we shall reap...." The image here is of a farm, and if there is one worker who knows what it means to stay on the job, it is the farmer. He must prepare the soil, sow the seed, pull the weeds, water the plants, and wait patiently for the harvest.

The farmer has no guaranteed harvest, but the Christian worker is promised a harvest "in due season." There are seasons to the Lord's work—times of plowing and planting, times of watering and cultivating, times of reaping. The wise worker must know what season it is and work accordingly. When we work together with the Lord, he is the one who "gives the increase" (1 Cor. 3:5–9).

The "due season" is not always at the end of the meeting, or even at the close of the church year. Jesus told us that "the harvest is the end of the age..." (Matt. 13:39). We may not see the results of our labors today or even next year, but we will see them when we stand before the Lord. Like the farmer, we must sow and water by faith, trusting the Lord to cause growth in his time.

Yes, it is always "too soon" to quit. We must be on guard and watch lest we start to "grow weary while doing good." If we keep in mind the *privilege* of serving Christ and believe his *promise* of the harvest, we will be able to guard against the *peril* of weariness, so as to "keep on keeping on" until he returns.

A survey published by a national retail sales organization revealed that 48 percent of salesmen in the United States quit after their first visit, while 25 percent called a second time before quitting. Only 15 percent made three visits—and then they gave up! The remaining 12 percent kept on calling— and they did 80 percent of the total business!

God's business is even more important, so it is *always* too soon to quit!

33
When God Works, We Work!
Philippians 2:12–18

"...work out your own salvation with fear and trembling; for it is God who works in you both to will and to do for His good pleasure" (vv. 12–13). Paul wrote these words to a local congregation. The pronouns are plural because he was exhorting all of the people. He wanted the church in Philippi *as a whole* to do the will of God, to "work out" God's purposes as he "worked in" their lives. Each local church must follow this example and "work out" the ministry God places before its membership. While all churches are alike in some respects, in others they must be different. Every local assembly has a special purpose to fulfill in God's time, by God's power, and for God's glory. It is dangerous for churches to imitate one another, because what is successful in one place may not be successful elsewhere.

No congregation can "work out" this divine plan unless the divine power is "worked in." God works in his people when they yield to him and genuinely want to do his will. He works in us when we pray, when we worship him, and when we open our hearts and minds to his Word. Christian service does not really mean that we work *for* the Lord, but

124

that he works in us and through us to accomplish his plan (Eph. 2:10).

This raises an important question. How can we tell when God is at work in our fellowship? In these verses, Paul answers that question by giving us the characteristics of the church in which God truly is at work:

There is an attitude of reverence that leads to obedience (v. 12). If people are serious about the things of the Lord, there is first a sincere desire to know God's will for the church and then—having discovered it—to do it "with fear and trembling." When God is at work in our lives, we want his will more than anything else, and we do his will because we love him and long to glorify him.

As you read the Scriptures, you discover that God's servants recognized the seriousness of their calling. They did not take lightly the responsibility of serving the Lord. If we are careless about our ministry, it is a sure sign that God is not at work. If we lack the "fear and trembling" that ought to mark Christian service, another power is at work in our midst—and that can lead to spiritual defeat. Christian service is joyful, but at the same time it is serious.

There is harmony among God's people (v. 14). If the Lord is at work in our fellowship, we will stop "murmuring and disputing" among ourselves. Instead, we will be praising him, rejoicing at the privilege of service, and doing all we can to help and encourage one another.

"Murmuring" was one of the chief sins of Israel as they journeyed to the Promised Land. They were experts at negative thinking! In spite of all the blessings God gave them, they grumbled about the way he led them and the way he fed them. They especially complained about the leaders he gave them. Instead of looking by faith to the future, they repeatedly wanted to go back to Egypt. Very few of the things done for them, either by God or Moses, were acceptable to them. They were a nation of complainers!

When God is at work in our midst, we do not complain. Instead, we give thanks for all that he does. Murmuring and disputing will have no place in our hearts or at our meetings if God is at work. Paul warns the Corinthians not to imitate Israel and murmur against the Lord (1 Cor. 10:10). God disciplined them—and he may discipline us.

We will have a clear witness to the lost (vv. 15–16). After all, is it not the major ministry of the church to witness to a lost world? If all we are doing is serving our own membership and maintaining an institution, then God is not truly at work among us.

We live in a distorted world, and the church must be "straight" when it comes to godly living. Standards have been so twisted by society that it is difficult to get people to commit themselves to what is right and what is wrong. God's people must be "children of God without fault," good examples of what it means to be a Christian, a disciple of Jesus Christ.

We must be shining lights in a dark world, "in the midst of a crooked and perverse generation." Too often the church is a mirror that only reflects the world around it, when the church ought to be a

126

bright beacon that illuminates the darkness and reveals the Lord Jesus Christ.

When God is at work, we are faithful witnesses, "holding fast the word of life...." We live in a distorted world, a dark world—a dead world that desperately needs God's Word of life. If God is working in us and through us, we will be faithful witnesses who present the saving message of Christ to those around us.

We will rejoice at opportunities to sacrifice for the Lord (vv. 17–18). These two verses are about sacrifice—and yet Paul mentions the idea of "joy" four times! The image is that of the priest offering a "drink offering" along with the burnt offering. Just as a cup of wine—a symbol of life—is poured out for God, Paul rejoiced at the opportunity to pour out his life for the sake of the Philippian believers. They were the burnt offering and he was the drink offering.

The well-known British preacher John Henry Jowett once said, "Ministry that costs nothing accomplishes nothing." He was right! If our service for the Lord is casual and easy, then it is not service at all. When God is at work in us, there is a price to pay; and we will rejoice in paying it! Our concern will not be for ourselves, but for others.

What a privilege it is to have God at work in us and through us! But what a tremendous responsibility it is! Let us take spiritual inventory to make sure that these four characteristics are found in our fellowship. Do we have an attitude of reverence? Is there harmony among us as we serve together? Do we have a strong witness to the lost? Are we willing to sacrifice?

127

34
The Highest Praise
Philippians 2:25

The baseball player who makes the fewest errors at his position receives a Golden Glove Award. An outstanding actor can win a Tony, Emmy, or Oscar. Scientists who produce deep insights receive the Nobel Prize. Soldiers who exhibit great courage receive the Congressional Medal of Honor. Authors who produce great literature are recognized by a Pulitzer Prize. The common element in these examples is that they are the highest form of praise that can be awarded in their fields.

There is nothing wrong with wanting to be "the best" in whatever we attempt. But here we are, preparing to do God's business. How do we measure "the best" in serving the Lord? In Philippians 2:25 we meet Epaphroditus. The terms Paul used to describe him illustrate the kind of person who receives the highest praise in God's work.

Paul introduced him as "Epaphroditus, my brother." The church began using the terms "brother" and "sister" quite early; it reminded all believers that they belonged to the family of God. Paul and Epaphroditus each trusted Jesus Christ as their Savior, both called God their "Father"—and so they were brothers.

All Christians are brothers, but some seem to radiate a spirit of familial warmth and love more than others. When Paul described his friend, the first thing he thought to say was, "He's a brother!" "Beloved, let us love one another..." wrote John (1 John 4:7). That bond of love makes us brothers.

Next, Epaphroditus is called a "fellow worker." He had come to bring a gift to Paul in prison from the church in Philippi. Once he found Paul, he worked with the apostle in whatever way he could. Some people just stand and *watch* folks work. Not Epaphroditus; he got busy! Some people go through life creating work for others, but Epaphroditus helped to get the work done.

There is an old saying that "some folks are like blisters; they don't show up until the work is done." As we go about God's business, let's not look for ways to avoid sharing the work load; let us find ways to reduce each person's burden by apportioning the duties among many.

Then Paul calls Epaphroditus a "fellow soldier." Paul was fighting great spiritual battles in serving the Lord, and he was glad for reinforcements. Heed a word of wisdom: "Be kind, because everyone you meet is fighting a battle." Our weapons in spiritual warfare are the Word of God and prayer. Epaphroditus probably prayed with Paul and encouraged him from the Scriptures.

When you are fighting a battle as a Christian, there is nothing more discouraging than to have a fellow believer offer criticism or advice as a spectator. What really lifts us up is when someone joins us and says, "I'm on *your* side." It gives us courage and strength to keep fighting. Quitting is easy; having a fellow soldier renews our determination to win the victory.

Finally, Paul calls Epaphroditus a "minister to my need." The Philippian church had sent a gift to help meet Paul's material needs, and Paul was blessed by it. His thank-you to them is beautiful (4:10–20). But Epaphroditus also ministered to Paul spiritually, and he seems to have had an ability to sense where Paul was hurting or weak. Then he helped to heal the wound by his encouragement.

Everyone we meet has needs. We need the sensitivity the Holy Spirit imparts, so we can lovingly meet those needs. When a believer allows God to show his love through their lives, God can do mighty things. As we seek to do God's work, we must bear in mind that ministry is not only something done to *us*, it is also something we do for others.

These are the qualities that earn the highest praise in God's service: showing Christian love, sharing the work load, standing in the battle, seeking to meet needs. Epaphroditus did not seek or receive a lot of recognition; he just quietly lived for the Lord Jesus. Being a servant and going unrecognized rarely brings much public commendation. But, in God's eyes, to serve as Epaphroditus did earns the *highest* praise—and that is what really counts!

35

Measured
by the Gospel
Colossians 1:3–8

As Paul began his letter to the Christians in Colossae, he gave thanks for them, and for the way they first responded to the "good news" of the gospel. It had transformed their lives, and molded them into a faithful church.

Someone said that for today's Christians the "good news" is no longer good, nor is it news. We have grown accustomed to the gospel, but it should never be routine for a child of God. Some believers treat their salvation like a consolation prize: if they get nothing else out of life, at least they will go to heaven. That God loves us, that Christ died for our sins on the cross, that we have eternal life—all this should thrill us every day!

Our new life in Christ began when we responded by faith to the gospel. No longer "babes in Christ," we still want to grow and mature as Christians, but we cannot leave the gospel behind! In fact, as we live for the Lord we are constantly being measured by the gospel. Let us apply this truth in two areas.

First, our church itself is measured by the gospel. As Paul reviewed the early days of the Colossian church, he touched on several influences the gospel should exert on the fellowship of believers. We can frame them as questions and test our own church by the answers.

1. *Are we true to the gospel message?* The gospel had come to the Colossians (v. 6), and they were proclaiming it as they had learned it. Some Christians think that being spiritually "deep" means leaving the simple truths behind. Actually, things that can be simply stated are often the most profound—such as the words "I love you." We need to be sure that the words that first brought us to Christ are still presented—in the pulpit, the Sunday-school classroom, the Bible-study group. The gospel is a source of God's grace, and we must be true to its message.

2. *Are we bearing fruit and increasing?* The message of salvation is not sterile or stagnant. It produces life by "bringing forth fruit" (v. 6). Are we seeing people come to Christ through the different ministries of our church?

3. *Are we a loving church family?* Paul had been told of the love demonstrated in the Colossian church (v. 8), and that love was a result of their response to the gospel. When we are mutually concerned about winning the lost and sharing our faith, it produces a harmony within the body that prevents unkindness.

Church leaders make a lot of decisions about budgets, staff, programs, services, and curriculum. In making those decisions, we have to consider whether they will further the gospel—because our church is evaluated in the light of its truths.

The second application of this passage is to our personal lives, which are also measured by the gospel. A church is made up of individuals, and God will hold us to account for what we have done with the gospel message. Our responsibility here is threefold:

First, we are responsible for *what* we have heard. The Colossians "heard...the word of the truth of the gospel" (v. 5), and what they heard affected the way they lived. They began the process of growing toward maturity. Is what you have heard becoming ingrained in your daily life?

Second, we are also responsible for *sharing* what we have heard. The Colossians did not keep the gospel to themselves. They shared it, and there was fruit and increase (v. 6). The gospel is worth possessing, and it is worth passing on.

Third, we are responsible to *love*. Christian love is inclusive—"for all the saints" (v. 4)—and is produced by the Holy Spirit (v. 8). The gospel reveals how much God loves us; and God's love in us enables us to be loving. A Christian who is close to God's heart will not be critical or unkind. But if we begin to take the gospel for granted, we may lose some of the energizing power of our "first love."

We are being measured by the gospel. Don't be nervous about that, as though God were looking over your shoulder all the time. But let us take seriously our accountability as a church, and as individuals, to the truth that is still "good news."

36

Think of It as Ministry

Colossians 4:7–14

Every successful leader was helped to succeed by the people who labored with him or her. Napoleon was a highly competent general—but his soldiers made him great. An athlete may be a superstar—but he must work with the rest of the team. Paul is a familiar figure to us as a great Christian—but Paul had a loyal group of people who sustained his efforts. In fact, much of what Paul was able to accomplish happened because of his support team.

Although the people who labor behind the scenes rarely get headlines, their work is just as valid as the accomplishments of the people who are recognized. We know who Paul was and what he did. Do you know Tychicus, and Aristarchus, and Epaphras? They are mentioned only briefly in the New Testament, but what they did was vital to Paul's ministry.

The lesson of this passage is simply that ministry takes many forms. Paul wrote many of the books of the New Testament, planted many churches, preached great sermons, and endured strong opposition. But that is not all there is to ministry. In Colossians 4:7–14, we are introduced to some special people who labored with Paul behind the scenes. Let us meet some of them and discover some ministries we can perform:

In verses 7–9, we meet Tychicus, who had served faithfully with Paul. He helped deliver the offering from the Asian churches to Jerusalem (Acts 20:4) and was Paul's representative and message bearer to several churches (cf. Eph. 6:21–22).

For Paul, Tychicus performed *the ministry of assistance.* When Paul could not visit the established churches, he needed someone to keep them informed (v. 7, 9). He was going to visit the Colossian church and report on what was happening with Paul. Tychicus had proved he could be trusted, and Paul depended on him often for assistance. Maybe you cannot teach, but you could be a teacher's aide. You may be unable to join the mission field, but you could correspond with missionaries. Each of us can help someone else somewhere. Look around your church, your neighborhood—who can you help? That's the ministry of assistance.

Tychicus also had *a ministry of encouragement* (v. 8). His visit to Colossae would strengthen the believers there. It would "comfort" them. In fact, that's what encouragement is—standing beside someone to help, sharing your strength with them.

Everyone needs encouragement. Even the strongest, most dedicated saints have times when the burden is so heavy that quitting is a temptation. God can use *us* to lighten the load and brighten the darkness of despair.

There are many ways to be an encourager. Send a card to a shut-in. Greet someone with a warm handshake or hug. (Church is the only place where some folks ever get a hug.) Offer a sincere compliment, or just be a good listener. Paul could not have done his work so well if people had not encouraged him. Look for ways to be a minister of encouragement.

We are introduced to Epaphras in verse 12. He was from the Colossian church and had come to visit Paul. In fact, it may have been the report he gave to Paul about the Colossian church that prompted Paul to write this letter. The one characteristic mentioned about Epaphras is that he was a man of prayer. He had a powerful *ministry of prayer* for the Colossian Christians, and most likely for Paul, too.

Only eternity can fully reveal just how significant our prayers of intercession for other Christians are. And prayer requires effort. We read that Epaphras was "laboring fervently" in his prayers—he no doubt tired himself out interceding for others. Never underestimate the power of prayer!

We cannot all teach or preach, but we all can pray for those who do. If God has not called you to serve as a missionary, you can pray for your church's missionary family. The problem is, prayer just doesn't seem like we are doing very much. The world at large notices and rewards visible action, not contemplation. But prayer is one of the most powerful activities we can engage in! Make the most of the ministry of prayer.

In closing this letter, Paul passes along greetings from the physician Luke (v. 14). We know Luke as the writer of both a synoptic Gospel and the Book of Acts. He traveled with Paul, and some think he may have been Paul's physician. There was obviously a close bond between Paul and

Luke, because Paul calls him "beloved." Luke was a friend to Paul, and it seems Paul did not have many close friends. Luke illustrates to us the *ministry of friendship.*

A friend is someone who shares the burdens with you, who helps you fight the battle. Luke was with Paul in prison and even suffered shipwreck with Paul (Acts 27). Luke was loyal to Paul and a dependable companion. Near the end of Paul's ministry, when everyone else was gone, Paul could write: "Only Luke is with me..." (2 Tim. 4:11).

Is there someone you should befriend? Someone who needs a good listener, another person to support, someone who won't be defensive or critical? God's people need each other. We are not to be Lone Rangers. We accomplish so much more for the Lord when we have someone to share the load.

Ministry takes many forms—and every form of ministry is important. Widen your scope of ministry and servanthood. Be willing to help, to encourage, to pray, to be a friend—just think of it as being involved in the total ministry of Christ.

37

When Things Are Shaking
Hebrews 12:25–29

The Christians who originally received the Epistle to the Hebrews were not having an easy time of it. These were Jewish believers struggling against the strong pull of their old religion. They had been persecuted for their faith, and some had even been imprisoned. These Hebrew Christians were strongly tempted to go back to the "good old days," to minimize their faith in Christ and enjoy peace and security again.

What was God's response to this situation? *He started to shake things!* Why? So that these believers would learn the difference between the temporary and the permanent. In a few years, the Jewish nation would be scattered throughout the Roman Empire, and Jerusalem and the temple would be destroyed. God's plan was to remove the things that could be shaken, so that "the things which cannot be shaken may remain" (v. 27). He was showing them the difference between the worldly scaffolding and the permanent spiritual temple he was building.

Our situation may not exactly parallel that of these Hebrews, but we are nevertheless living in a time when many things are being "shaken." And the very nature of change is changing! It used to be that changes came gradually, and we had the opportunity to examine and assimilate them. But that is not the case today. Changes take place so fast and with such force that we often feel like ducking! How easy it would be to imitate these Hebrews and start thinking about retreating into some safe refuge—and let the rest of the world go by. We long for the relative calm of the traditional past.

But, if we retreat, we will disobey the Lord and miss the very opportunities for ministry that he is giving to us. In times of radical change, we as Christians have the privilege of telling people that there are some things that cannot change:

God's Word does not change. God is still speaking, if only we will listen (v. 25). If we build our lives and ministries on the constantly changing philosophies and theories of this world, we will be confused and defeated. But if we build on the eternal Word of God, the changes around us will not be a threat to us. God's Word has remained true and effective throughout all generations, and it will not fail us today. "Heaven and earth will pass away, but My words will by no means pass away" (Matt. 24:35).

One of the wonderful characteristics of the Bible is its timelessness. The principles and promises of God's Word are not limited by time or culture. The believers in the early church had only the Old Testament to guide them, and yet the Spirit led them to make right decisions. Today, we have an entire Bible, and we must be careful to let God direct us from his Word. The writer warns us that we must listen to God's voice and obey it, if we expect him to bless.

139

God's disciplines do not change. "See that you do not refuse Him who speaks" (v. 25). Why this warning? Because those who refuse God's Word are disciplined and judged by the Lord. "But we live in this age of grace," someone might argue, "and in the age of grace, God deals with us in love, as with children." But that is one of the key themes of Hebrews. It is *because* we are his dear children that our Father must chasten us when we rebel against him. In fact, his fatherly chastening is proof that he loves us (Heb. 12:5–6). Whether under the Old Covenant or the New, God can never condone sin.

A church member once criticized her pastor because he had been preaching about the sins of God's people. "After all," she argued, "sin in the life of a Christian is different from sin in the life of an unsaved person."

"Yes," replied the pastor, "it's worse!"

It is easy for us to get "soft on sin," not only in our own lives, but also in the life of the church. A defiled ministry is a defeated ministry. Our standards can gradually deteriorate until we awaken one day to discover that we have no Christian standards at all! We need to heed God's Word and remind ourselves that his loving disciplines do not change.

God's kingdom does not change. We belong to "a kingdom which cannot be shaken" (v. 28). God has always had his people in this world, and his people have always had their security in the Lord. "Lord, You have been our dwelling place in all generations" (Ps. 90:1). If we build on the things of this world, our work will not last; if we build on the Rock, in obedience to his Word, our ministry will last forever (Matt. 7:24–27).

140

How tragic it is when spiritual leaders spend more time on the temporary—the shaking scaffolding—than they do on the eternal. In the midst of a shaking world, we must lay hold of those things that cannot shake and cannot be destroyed. How do we do this? By obeying the admonitions that conclude this passage of Scripture:

"Let us have grace…" (v. 28). We cannot acceptably serve the God of grace apart from the grace of God. None of us is worthy or adequate to serve God. We desperately need his sufficient grace!

Let us *"serve God acceptably with reverence and godly fear"* (v. 28). Serving God is serious business. We must not be solemn and lose our sense of humor, but neither should we be careless and flippant about the Master's work. "Godly fear" implies that we respect God and acknowledge him as Lord, that we take seriously the tasks he gives us to do.

"For our God is a consuming fire" (v. 29). What will be left? Treasures that are purified, or ashes that announce that we built carelessly and cheaply? One day the fire will test our work (1 Cor. 3:10–15).

When things are shaking, it is easy to be tempted to use cheap shortcuts and to do our work carelessly. Let us be sure to lay hold of the things that do not shake, so that we may build on God's plan in a way that glorifies him.

38
We Have to Show God!
I John 4:7–21

As the familiar hymn declares, "Jesus loves me, this I know...." And we're so glad about it! The longer we walk with Christ, the more we appreciate Calvary and the empty tomb. Our church, our homes and families, our jobs—all are evidences that God loves us. And the surety of that love is something worth celebrating!

Knowing that God loves us raises a related question: How does God know that *we* love *him*? You might say, "But God knows everything, so he knows we love him." True. But even a man who is sure of his wife's love for him wants to hear "I love you" and be shown that he is loved. If we do not show our love for God, we really do not know him (v. 8). How do we demonstrate our love for God? This passage suggests three ways:

We show our love for God by our confession of Christ (vv. 14–15). The Father sent his Son as a gift to us. When we receive Christ, the Son of God becomes our Savior and gives us eternal life. As we grow to know Jesus better, we learn more about God's love through his Son. When we confess Jesus as Lord and Savior, we are showing that God abides in us, and that we love him.

Now, many of us *say* we believe in Jesus, but our words must be tested by our lives. People who truly love God have staked their lives on the fact that Jesus died for their sins and rose again to give them eternal life. Their conduct shows they are motivated by a desire to please and glorify God. Their confession of Christ goes beyond mere words; it affects values, attitudes, and behavior. There is a consistency between profession and practice.

How much does Jesus Christ mean to you? Do your actions reflect and support your words about Jesus? Is it important to you to confess Christ in such a way that it reveals a deep love for God?

We can show our love for God by our confidence in him (v. 16). If we love God, we will be sure of his love for us. Love and trust always go together and produce commitment. Since God's commitment to us was made through Jesus at Calvary, we have no doubts about the depths of his love.

Imagine a husband and wife constantly asking each other, "Do you *really* love me?" Sometimes a wife will ask her husband, "Do you love me?" not because she doubts his love, but because she wants to hear it affirmed. A constant questioning betrays a lack of trust, and love cannot exist without trust. If we love God, we will not doubt his love for us. We will accept the fact that we are the object of the Father's love and will bask in the glow of that assurance. Of course, we will not take his love for granted either—it will be a precious treasure.

Some people, though, are unsure of God's love. They go through life afraid that God is going to punish them. It is tragic when a child is terrified of a parent, believing that no matter how hard he tries to please, he will still be hurt. God is not like that! As Jesus is the beloved of the Father, so we are loved by the heavenly Father (v. 17). He will never harm us, and he desires only what is good for his children: "There is no fear in love..." (v. 18).

We do not have to wonder about God's love for us. His Word affirms it (vv. 16, 19), and the Holy Spirit witnesses to it within us (Rom. 8:16). Jesus demonstrated God's love at Calvary (John 3:16). If we love God, we will be confident of his love for us.

We can show our love for God by concern for his people (vv. 20–21). If we love our Father in heaven, we will love our brothers and sisters in Christ. It is easy to *say* we love God. After all, he is invisible, and seemingly there is no objective way of disproving the claim. But God gave us a test: If you do not love the brother you can see, you do not love the Father you cannot see (v. 20). If you cannot show love for your fellow believer, maybe you are not a believer at all!

All through the New Testament, there is a strong emphasis on Christians who demonstrated their love for one another. Our tangible, visible signs of love show that we acknowledge God's presence. But when a Christian avoids true fellowship with God's people, when he can only offer criticisms, when he uses others' failings as an excuse for non-involvement —well, there probably is no love relationship with God in that person's heart.

Take a quick inventory, to see if we are concerned about God's people in this church. Which is more frequent here—compliments or criticism? Do we exercise forgiveness, or nurse our wounds? When we disagree, do we build walls, not bridges? Do we care for everyone, or are we indifferent to some?

We need to show God that we love him. So let us love each other. Maybe we need to exchange words of forgiveness. Perhaps we should offer words of praise and encouragement. Maybe just sharing a holy handshake will show our love!

We do not question God's love for us—we rejoice in it. But sometimes we may give God reason to question our love for him. He continues to show us his great love. Let us prove that love is reciprocated in our words, attitudes, and actions!

39
Profit and Loss
2 John 8–9

God's work is always in jeopardy, and those of us who are leaders must stay alert to the dangers. Sometimes Satan comes as a lion to devour (1 Peter 5:8), and at other times he comes as a serpent to deceive (2 Cor. 11:3). No matter what Satan may attempt, we must be "sober" and "vigilant" to protect God's work and see to it that the ministry to his workers goes on with blessing.

In these two verses, the aged apostle John pointed out two special threats to the church: the danger of losing what we have gained, and the danger of making gains that are really losses. You and I certainly need discernment and wisdom to detect these dangers and overcome the enemy.

As to the first danger, John tells us, "Look to yourselves, that we not lose those things we have worked for, but that we receive a full reward" (v. 8). Sometimes we are so anxious to move forward in God's work that we fail to conserve and protect the blessings we have already received.

When we consider some of the images of the church given in the New Testament, this warning becomes even more arresting. The church is a spiritual family, and we must take care of the new

146

"babies" that God gives us. Who would think of bringing a baby into the world and then abandoning it? The church is a field (1 Cor. 3:6–9), and we must cultivate the seeds and pull up the weeds if we expect to have a good harvest. The church is God's temple (1 Cor. 3:9–17), and if a building is not kept in good repair, it falls down.

Finally, the church is also God's spiritual army (2 Tim. 2:3–4), and we must take care lest we win the battle and end up losing the war. If a conquering army fails to keep the enemy under control, all the new territory gained will eventually be lost. Every general knows how important it is to leave troops behind to guard the gains.

Who is to blame when the church loses its gains? *We* are! John did not blame Satan; he wrote, "Look to yourselves...." If we are losing our gains, we have nobody to blame but ourselves. As spiritual leaders, we must guard God's work and see to it that we are not taking two steps forward and sliding three steps backward. If that is happening, not only is God's work in danger, but we are in danger of losing our reward.

The second danger is that of making gains that are really losses. The New International Version of verse 9 reads, "Anyone who runs ahead and does not continue in the teaching of Christ does not have God...." This is a warning against the "progressive theology" that abandons "the faith that was once for all entrusted to the saints" (Jude 3, NIV) and ends up denying Jesus Christ. Over the centuries, more than one ministry has gone backward by trying to move "forward" in developing a so-called up-to-date doctrinal position.

To be sure, there is always more to be learned

from the Bible! And the unchanging Word of God must constantly be related to whatever new insight men discover in Scripture. But to go beyond the fundamental truths that the church holds dear is to make "gains" that are really losses. We must know the truth, live the truth, defend the truth, and share the truth with others. But we must never go *beyond* that truth.

God's people certainly want to see God's work move forward. We want to see the family grow, but we must be sure we are caring for the new babies properly. We want the field to produce a great harvest, but this means caring for the field, lest the weeds move in and take over. The Christian army must conquer new territory, but let us be sure we hold on to the territory we already have, lest we turn victories into defeats.

This is why God's work is so important, and why it demands the very best that we can give it. We are on guard duty for God, staying alert to protect our gains and rejecting profits that are really losses. If you ask, "... who is sufficient for these things?" (1 Cor. 2:16), the answer is clear: "... our sufficiency is from God" (2 Cor. 3:5).

40

On Being Faithful
Selected Texts

It is not the person who is eloquent, highly trained, or multigifted that God specially blesses. It is the person who is "faithful."

More than twenty times in the New Testament the word *faithful* is applied to people who serve the Lord. But what does that mean? Faithfulness has to be more than mouthing a creed or claiming to love Jesus. Words are too easy. No, faithfulness to God is tested in the daily course of living. As we search the Scriptures, we discover several marks of the faithful Christian:

Faithfulness to the church is one sign we are looking for. Reflect on Hebrews 10:24–25: "And let us consider how to stimulate one another to love and good deeds, not forsaking our own assembling together, as is the habit of some, but encouraging one another..." (NASB). The church is God's family, and we belong to it because of what Christ did for us on the cross. Out of gratitude and obedience to Christ, we should be loyal to our church.

Church leaders certainly ought to make it a top priority to attend services, not only for the spiritual benefits, but because they set an example for the flock. (This does not mean that each Christian has

149

to be in church every time the doors are open!) Attending faithfully accomplishes several purposes. It encourages all those who come to worship and pray, affirming to each person present that he or she is not alone in the world. And it stimulates us to do good and show Christian love to our fellow worshipers.

There are other ways to be faithful to the church. Praying regularly for the pastor and other leaders is one. Another is to be a systematic giver. Holding an office in a church organization, or using your gifts in one of the church programs, also expresses faithfulness to the church.

Faithfulness with one's time is a second mark of the faithful believer. In Ephesians 5:16, we are advised about "making the most of every opportunity" (NIV). Time is a gift to us from God. Since we cannot take tomorrow for granted, we must focus on today. Life goes by so quickly, yet we measure it in years. Each day, each moment, needs to be seized like a precious treasure and used in the best way possible. "So teach us to number our days..." says the psalmist (90:12).

Time brings a responsibility. Time is a nonrenewable resource, so we must use it wisely. Some people kill time, others waste it. God's people are supposed to redeem time, to use it in ways that bear fruit for eternity. Time is the great revealer in that it shows our true character, our maturity, our values. So often we hear the complaint or excuse that "I don't have time." But we can always find time for what is most important to us. People who love God will be faithful to redeem the time available for the Lord's service.

150

Faithfulness with material resources is another mark of the faithful Christian. Jesus asks in Luke 16:11: "If therefore you have not been faithful in the use of unrighteous mammon, who will entrust the true riches to you?" (NASB). All we possess comes from God, and how we use those resources is a measure of our spiritual commitment.

Money and worldly possessions are but tools to build with, and God expects us to use these material things of life to gain eternal blessings (Luke 16:9). When we think of stewardship, we usually think of the 10 percent that we ought to return to God. But the acid test is how we use the other 90 percent!

Faithfulness in small things also gives evidence of commitment. Luke 16:10 is to the point: "He who is faithful in a very little thing is faithful also in much; and he who is unrighteous in a very little thing is unrighteous also in much" (NASB). How we react in a crisis reveals our character; how we respond to daily responsibilities is also a measure of character. When you promise to pray for someone, do you follow through? Do you keep your other promises? Do you perform those small, thankless tasks, even when no one but God is watching?

Our faithfulness in little things determines our readiness to be responsible for larger matters. With little things, God is testing to see if we can be trusted. In the parable of the talents (Luke 19:11–27), the servant who invested his ten talents became ruler of ten cities. The servant who did nothing but hide his portion for safekeeping lost all he had. Always be faithful to every responsibility, for you never know when you are being measured for a greater position!

One day we will give account to God for our lives. God will not be looking at attendance pins or softball trophies. He will be evaluating our faithfulness by our commitment to his church, our responsible use of time, our stewardship and servanthood.